KERRY BROWN is Professor of Chinese Studies and Director of the Lau China Institute at King's College London, and Associate on the Asia Programme at Chatham House. Prior to this he was Professor of Chinese Politics and Director of the China Studies Centre at the University of Sydney. With 25 years' experience of China, he has worked in education, business and government, including a term as First Secretary at the British Embassy in Beijing. He has written on China for the *London Review of Books*, *The Diplomat* and *Foreign Policy*, as well as for many international and Chinese media outlets. He is the bestselling author of *The New Emperors: Power and the Princelings in China* (2014), *CEO, China: The Rise of Xi Jinping* (2016) and *China's World: What Does China Want?* (2017), all published by I.B.Tauris. His other books include *Contemporary China* (2013), *Friends and Enemies: The Past, Present and Future of the Communist Party of China* (2009) and *Struggling Giant: China in the 21st Century* (2007).

THE WORLD
ACCORDING TO XI

Everything You Need to Know
About the New China

Kerry Brown

I.B. TAURIS

LONDON · NEW YORK

Published in 2018 by
I.B.Tauris & Co. Ltd
London • New York
www.ibtauris.com

ISBN: 978 1 78831 328 5
eISBN: 978 1 78672 429 8
ePDF: 978 1 78673 429 7

A full CIP record for this book is available from the British Library
A full CIP record is available from the Library of Congress
Library of Congress Catalog Card Number: available

Typeset by Tetragon, London
Printed and bound in the U.S.A. by Berryville Graphics Inc.,
Berryville, Virginia

To Rana Mitter,
with admiration and thanks.

CONTENTS

ACKNOWLEDGEMENTS

First of all, I would like to thank Tomasz Hoskins and his colleagues at I.B.Tauris for their continuing support.

This book would not be what it is without those responsible for the nuts and bolts in its journey to publication, and for this I am very grateful to Sarah Terry for her careful copy-editing and attention to detail, Alex Billington at Tetragon for the high-quality typesetting and production, and Alex Middleton for the proofreading.

INTRODUCTION

On 18 October 2017, Xi Jinping stood up in the Great Hall of the People in Beijing as Party secretary of the Communist Party of China to deliver the political report on behalf of the Central Committee to the delegates of the 19th Party Congress. The hall was full. On his left and right sat Jiang Zemin and Hu Jintao, the former holders of the position he now fills.

His speech lasted 3 hours and 23 minutes. This was a mammoth oration, even for a country which doesn't pressure its high-level officials to watch the clock while speaking. His address referred to the great mission his nation had embarked on: to be rejuvenated, to be a major power – perhaps *the* major power – of the modern era. It was in many ways a fitting commemoration of the country's remarkable resurrection, a country which, within living memory, had experienced famine, international and civil war, revolution and endless political power struggles and distractions. Finally, the promise given by the founding leader of the Communist Party in 1949 when the People's Republic had been founded – to have China's dignity restored to it after a century of victimisation and bullying by others and allow the Chinese people to stand tall – was coming to pass. And it would be under Xi's watch that this promise would come to fruition.

The consensus from around the world on this congress was that it had finally consolidated Xi's power. He was master now of all he surveyed. Since his appointment in 2012, he had come to dominate the Party via its anti-corruption struggle and a series of personnel moves he had spearheaded. But his reach seemed far beyond this. His visits abroad to 50 countries during his period in power have demonstrated that he is speaking not just to China, but to the whole world. In October 2017, during congress proceedings, *The Economist* magazine's front cover carried the simple image of Xi with the statement 'The World's Most Powerful Man'.

Xi's power has become a widespread obsession. Former US president Barack Obama blithely stated that Xi had consolidated power faster and more comprehensively than probably anybody since Deng Xiaoping. Others were keen to join in the praise, some even saying that he was only equalled by Mao. One commentator in Beijing outdid even this, telling me shortly before the congress that Xi's powers and ambitions transcend even those of the founding father, stating simply that Xi wants to rule the world.

This seems hyperbolic. As outsiders, it is interesting to note the way we like to relate Chinese leaders so closely to power. Our assessment of democratic leaders, on the other hand, is more nuanced: they have power, too, but only to a certain extent. There are limitations to what they can do, and their influence naturally ebbs and flows. The mighty today can be toppled after some mishap, as David Cameron found out in 2016 when, after having won the British election the year before, he was sidelined as a result of the Brexit referendum going against his expectations, and then simply removed from power, in the space of a few weeks.

In China we speak about Chinese leaders having a form of Chinese power. They don't hold elections. Their power looks purer and stronger. But anyone with even the most cursory knowledge of Chinese modern history since 1949 would know that Xi's China and that of Deng or Mao were very different places. Mao Zedong, leading a marginalised and divided guerrilla force, became ruler of the world's third-largest country in terms of territory, and was instrumental in campaigns and acts of war for two decades. He was present, with about a dozen other people, at the first ever congress in 1921. Mao's rise was on the back of violence, bloodshed and strife, in a society decimated by civil and international war. From 1949 until 1976, despite many ups and downs, he maintained his political dominance, never seriously threatened by any contender simply because of his status as the victor of the battles of the past. Deng Xiaoping had a different suite of attributes, but his impact might be judged by historians to have been even greater. Taking control of a China brought to its knees by Mao's economic illiteracy and love of class struggle and mass campaigns, Deng miraculously turned the whole country around, adopting ideas like foreign capital investment, a domestic market and entrepreneurialism, all of which had been anathema under Mao. His influence was never through formal positions of power, however. After 1978, for instance, he was never president, nor Party secretary, although he maintained leadership of the military until 1989. He simply had the political capital and credibility to make sure others followed his lead. Even well into his eighties, when his sole position was chair of the Chinese Contract Bridge Association, he was able to influence events.

In many ways, the China of today is the creation of Mao and Deng: Mao, who through brute use of violence and force gained power for the communists; and Deng, who reshaped the country and Party's strategy so that China became sustainable. These two leaders laid the tracks along which the country now travels. What links them despite their manifold differences is that they were both nationalists, leaders who believed in a strong, modernised, powerful China that would never again be a victim of foreign aggression and humiliation. There were significant differences, however, in how they wanted to achieve this aim. This commitment to national greatness is still important in today's China.

In this nationalist context, Xi Jinping's power can best be seen as on a continuum with his predecessors' power. He is following a tradition they set up, delivering the great nation Mao promised, largely in the way that Deng made clear would be most successful – through a focus on material power. In his own statements, Xi has gone out of his way to stress this continuity, accepting that he is simply the most recent iteration of this great tradition. His power is the power of this tradition, derived from the story first told in 1949 of the mission to ensure that Chinese people would have a voice and would never be forced to remain silent again. The hardest thing to understand about power in this context is that it is an attribute of a *system* rather than of a person. The person plays the tune, but others have all contributed to its composition. Were there no tune, there would be nothing to play. Were there no Party, or had there been no Mao or Deng, then Xi would be nothing. As I will explain, the power that Xi is ascribed and which he wields makes no sense outside this context.

The common assumption is that in 2017, Xi is halfway through his period in power. There are reasons to think that he may stay longer than this, and they will be looked at later. But this short book aims to give a 'halfway report'. I will attempt to unpack some of the things that make Xi noteworthy. Understanding his background is important – not just his individual background, but that of the milieu he grew up in. It is also crucial to understand his politics and ideology, or the politics and ideology of the Party under him. I hope in the next few chapters to set out, as clearly and accessibly as possible, who this politician is, what he is trying to do, what challenges face him and how successful he has been so far. Whatever the best way to understand Xi's power, he is a significant figure because he leads an immensely significant country, and deserves to be widely understood and thought about. I hope this book will help a little with that.

1

XI'S STORY

A book produced in July 2017 in Beijing carried the simple title *Xi Jinping Tells Stories*. Divided into two sections, covering stories about the outside world and those about China's domestic situation, it started with a tale borrowed from Mao Zedong – that of the foolish old man and the mountain. Exhaustively related during the Maoist era, it told of an old man who was trying to move a mountain to get a better view from his house. He was doing so, however, only with the aid of buckets. Observers laughed at him, saying he was doomed never to succeed. But he replied simply that if *he* didn't shift the earth, his children, grandchildren or great grandchildren would.

That sort of resilience was something that the Party, with its codes of selflessness under Mao Zedong, wanted to inculcate in society. The great project of modernising a country which had suffered so much, and fallen so far behind, was its most important mission right from the start. It was a mission that has connected the various phases of Party leadership since 1949. For the other tales contained in *Xi Jinping Tells Stories*, Xi used sources from abroad, and from the rich and endless inheritance of Chinese classical literature. As the national storyteller-in-chief, Xi was attempting to emulate Mao's ability to encapsulate complex stories in a simple format. The punchline to the story of the old man and the mountain was an uplifting one. God appeared, moved by the patience, faith and resilience of the old man. The mountains were shifted. Justice prevailed.

One of the most striking stories Xi has been telling since he came to power is his own. A book published in 2017 covered the era in which he lived in a cave in the remote Yan'an area in Shaanxi province – another parallel with the life of Mao. The message was simple: this was someone who had really lived among the people, who had experience of hardship, and through this had earned the right to speak about the things that affected all Chinese people. Xi was referred to as a 'peasant emperor' because he came from an elitist family but had been sent to the countryside during the Cultural Revolution, where he had experienced deprivation and hardship. Lee Kuan Yew, the late leader of Singapore, even went as far as to call him 'Asia's Nelson Mandela', while the foreign press referred dramatically to his time in the early 1970s as a pig farmer. This all conveyed the idea that somehow he had *earned* the right to occupy the high office he now holds.

This formal recognition of Xi's backstory was a radical departure for the Party. His immediate predecessor Hu Jintao had been the man from nowhere, someone who never once in public referred to anything remotely like a personal history. Even his precise place of birth was unclear. With Xi there was a conscious effort by the Party to make something of his story, using it to develop more of an emotional bond between the supreme leader and the Chinese people.

There are two components of the story Xi has been telling about himself: his own personal narrative, and that of the era of Chinese history he lived through. Xi's early years were spent in unusual circumstances, in the prelude to and aftermath of the strange, distorted period of the Cultural Revolution. This decade-long, complex movement remains an endless source of fascination for people both within and outside China. More than 50 years later, there is no easy interpretative framework into which it will fit; even those who lived through it are often unable to understand precisely what happened. The Cultural Revolution is regarded as either an inter-elite power struggle that went badly wrong, a whim of Mao's that careered out of control, or a profoundly significant spiritual holocaust for the Chinese people which led to the collapse of their values and world views. It is most probably a mixture of all of these things.

Xi's experience of this era was dominated by a power struggle among the elites – one that he had direct links with because of his family background. He was born in 1953, the son of Xi Zhongxun, a military leader and ally of Mao Zedong from the 1930s. Zhongxun had been vice premier with some responsibility for culture up to 1961, when he became embroiled in a dispute over unfavourable interpretations of a novel published that year. Caught on the wrong side of a political spat, he was placed under house arrest but saved from imprisonment, reportedly following a direct instruction by Mao. For almost the next two decades, he remained out of power, to all intents and purposes incarcerated. Over that period, his son is thought to have only seen him a few times.

For Xi, the second-oldest boy of seven children, the years when he was entering adolescence were the usual mixture of insecurity and bewildering personal changes. In 1966 he stayed on at an elite school next to the Zhongnanhai leadership compound, but he was then unceremoniously shipped down to the Yan'an area of northern Shaanxi province, joining a production brigade there. It seems that during this time he had contact with a figure who would be an elite leader alongside him later on – Wang Qishan. However, this period is romanticised in his current storytelling: both historical and contemporary testimonies from others who went through this process revealed an era that was often traumatising and alienating. Children from the city with no experience of rural life, and no useful local networks, were sent to areas which were mostly unable to look after themselves properly. Abuse and bullying were rife. Tales of resentful farmers and rural dwellers grudgingly looking after large numbers of people who were in their view pampered and mostly useless are plentiful. There is even a whole literature made up of testimonies about this unique phase in modern Chinese history in which the urbanisation process was reversed and cities shrunk rather than increased in size. It is called 'scar' or 'wounded' writing.

The contemporary hagiography of Xi's rural life tells us that he succeeded, gained the respect and admiration of the peasants he was living among, and managed to acquire a deep knowledge of the conditions in one of the most backward areas of the country. Whether this is accurate or not, this period would have undoubtedly had a huge impact on him. Even Deng Xiaoping, exiled to rural Jiangxi to work at a tractor factory around the same time and at a far more advanced stage in life, was profoundly changed by his experiences in this sort of community. For Deng, the poverty he saw in his sixth decade, after more than 40 years of working for the Party, was irrefutable evidence of communism's failure in China to do what it had set out to achieve – to improve the lives of rural workers. Almost three decades after socialism had first become the country's governing system, people in rural areas were experiencing widespread malnutrition, their living conditions were still very basic, and levels of backwardness were shocking. This was a moment of profound re-evaluation for Deng, and his experience of the period lay at the heart of his sponsorship of wholesale changes when he was in a position to support these after Mao's death in 1976.

For Xi, who was younger and more inexperienced, the impact of the things he saw in Shaanxi was different. But it has evidently endured. In 2017, even while lavishly praising the national rejuvenation that was taking place, Xi stated that poverty in China would be a thing of the past by 2020. And his domestic visits have included returning several times to what had been his rural base in the 1970s, and visits to similar villages. It is telling that the period he spent in this sort of community figures so prominently in official accounts of his life. Of the recent leaders of China since Deng, in many ways Xi is the one with the most authentic, best-known links to the countryside, and his use of this set of experiences aims to convey this.

Like many of the sent-down youths of the Cultural Revolution era, Xi's period of rustication ended almost as abruptly as it had begun, with his return to the capital in the mid-1970s to study engineering at Tsinghua University. The educational system had largely been crippled by internecine struggles and political turmoil throughout this period. Universities in Beijing had become hotbeds of leftist activism and rebellion. There was controversy after Xi's final elevation in 2012 about just how credible his entry to the elite Beijing-based university had been. A quota system existed for youths like him who had been sent to rural areas; his elite background may, ironically, have helped, even at a time when such things were regarded as a stigma. That Xi studied engineering nominally makes him a technocrat.

It is worth considering in a little more detail the meaning of the Cultural Revolution for people who like Xi came of age when the mass movement was at its height, and whose formative years were overshadowed by the events leading up to it and the developments which followed. In 2016, during the 50th anniversary of the issuance of the 16 July Notification – widely accepted as the official start of what is still called in domestic discourse in China the 'ten years of turbulence' – the sole event marking the occasion was an editorial in the *People's Daily*, the newspaper of the Party. The article decried, in standard terms, the loss of time and the destruction that the movement had involved. This has been the default attitude since the Party Resolution on the history of this era was issued in 1981. For Xi, his infrequent and brief mentions of the decade have been negative. For a leader often accused of being Maoist and having a similar cult of personality around him, it is odd that he and the Party propagandists have spoken little of his own direct experience of Maoism. Xi has displayed not a trace of nostalgia for this era, and yet in many ways it would have been the most powerful influence on him, with its mass adoration of a political figure, its extraordinary mobilisation of large parts of society, and the brief but intense and intoxicating fervour that it inspired.

One of the great dilemmas today for the Party as it looks back over this era is the simple but unpalatable fact that the Cultural Revolution was – at least while it was happening – a popular movement, and one that engaged the active involvement of millions of young Chinese people. It was also a moment when China, for the only time in its long history, was unified by a faith – that of Mao Zedong Thought. This ended up being a faith that failed. But it left a profound stain on people's memories. In Xi, for example, it gave him the world view of a victim rather than a victimiser. That has proved an asset. It means that his role is more complex: he is more a survivor of Mao than a diehard follower. His later commitment to Mao makes more sense if seen as a fidelity to a symbolic figure and to the creator of a body of ideas around sinified Marxism that are still seen as relevant. But as for Mao as a person, things are more complicated. The one fact widely known about Xi is that his father at least survived the Cultural Revolution and made a comeback in the late 1970s during the era of Dengist rehabilitation. In that sense he was spared. Many of his peers had perished. Xi the son stood on the outer circles of the Maoist fury, and saw even from there the intensity of its inner fire. That must have had a searing impact on him, and given him a resilience which is stressed in his official biography to this day. It also gave him an ability to observe ruthless procedures with equanimity – something that stood him in good stead when he was to observe the fall of his colleagues Bo Xilai and Zhou Yongkang years later. Mao was the greatest teacher and practitioner of the adage that in Chinese politics the winner takes all. In that sense, and perhaps only in that sense, Xi is a modern-day Maoist.

In Western politics, we seek signs of agency in our elite political leaders, moments that help to reveal their inner convictions – or lack of them. One of the main clues is their choice of which party to serve early in their careers. There are other moments along the way when they make choices, or betray inclinations, beliefs and ideas. In the one-party system in China, the choice is simple for anyone interested in organised politics – to join the Communist Party. The real question is why people want to get involved in politics at all, especially those from Xi's background. Politicians in the Party seem to have little choice over their actions. However, from his biography, we know of two key features which demonstrate Xi's free will. The first is the sheer number of attempts he made, ten in all, to join the Party before he was finally accepted in 1973. The second was his shift in the early 1980s from a military career to one in the civilian sphere. Once more, this seems to have been a personal choice. He worked from 1978 to 1982 as the secretary of Geng Biao, a member of the Central Military Commission and a key military figure. That should have set him up for a stellar career in the army, but he took the more elongated route through civilian, provincial administration and Party affairs from 1982 onwards. That involved once more leaving the confines of Beijing and heading to provincial China, first to Hebei around the capital, and then, from 1985, to Fujian. Military careers always carried status and influence in China, but they were never going to deliver major political clout. That Xi took this route might suggest that, even as early as this, he had a strategic vision of one day becoming an elite political figure. It certainly betrays an interest in the political realm and indicates some level of ambition.

In the years Xi was in the south-eastern coastal province of Fujian, it would have been difficult to imagine him having an easy route to Beijing and central leadership. Fujian was one of the most outward-looking provinces, and was starting to engage with Taiwanese businesses because of its proximity to the thriving capitalist and technologically advanced economy of the de facto independent island. Xi's 16 years here from 1985 form the backbone of his career before central leadership. It was here that he married Peng Liyuan, the famous singer and lieutenant general in the People's Liberation Army. Peng was his second wife, his first marriage having ended in divorce after his wife had moved to take up a diplomatic posting, accompanying her father to the UK. Peng is an important factor in Xi's development: firstly because until 2007 her profile was far higher than his (she was the star of China Central Television's annual New Year performance for many years), and secondly because his marriage to her was further demonstration that he was a member of the elite. Since 2007, she has figured increasingly as a source of background influence, possibly the first time since Mao that a top leader's spouse has been accorded a prominent public role. However, unlike the wife of Mao, the demagogue and leftist activist Jiang Qing, Peng's role has been far more benign.

The final position Xi took in Fujian, from 2000 to 2002, was as governor. Prior to this, in the late 1990s he completed a doctorate at Tsinghua University in law in the Marxism–Leninism Study Department. He also managed to survive one of the most extensive corruption scandals when a Fujian businessman, Lai Changxing, almost single-handedly managed to seduce every significant local leader with cash, sex or other inducements as part of a multi-billion-dollar smuggling racket. The fallout from the scandal led to Lai fleeing to Canada (before being extradited back to China over a decade later), and the disciplining of a whole generation of Fujian-based leaders. Based on Xi's official biography, and on statements he made at the time, he seems to have avoided the traps set for him. That is interesting in itself: the area was booming for much of the time he was there, making inducements almost irresistible to elite leaders and their personal networks. Again, was it a driving ambition that led Xi to be very cautious about his involvement with business networks? He certainly spoke as though he were someone with a clear divide in his head between the Party as a political entity and the commercial world developing around it. Perhaps more meaningfully, he also managed to keep his immediate family out of local business dealings. His sisters and his elder brother were uninvolved with any major companies in the areas where he worked. This was something that other elite leaders proved unable or unwilling to do (family ties, in a society orientated towards family networks, are the hardest to resist), and led to the fall of many of them.

Xi's first major promotion was in 2002, to the dynamic coastal province of Zhejiang, where he served in the top Party slot for five years. Around this time, he started to produce a blog, 'New Sayings from Zhejiang', about issues in the region – if not directly written by him, then ghostwritten with his close guidance. This was done under a pseudonym. His work in Zhejiang was relatively business-friendly, but not spectacular. He encouraged foreign investors to come in greater numbers to the mostly private sector-dominated area, and was present when Jack Ma started to develop a small internet start-up which eventually morphed into the mammoth that is Alibaba today. In the middle of the same decade, when speculation started about who might be Hu Jintao's successor, Xi's name figured as one among a set of younger, ambitious leaders – and not, perhaps, as the most compelling. It was therefore by no means a given that during the build-up to 2007 and the 17th Party Congress later that year that Xi would emerge in pole position.

The one significant clue that he might be on track for a major promotion came in 2007 with his brief tenure in Shanghai, the most dynamic of Chinese places, after the felling of Chen Liangyu, the Party head there, for corruption connected with the running of pension funds. As it had been for Jiang Zemin two decades previously, Shanghai proved to be a good stepping stone before going on to higher things. As a result of this period, there was little surprise when he emerged in October that year as the fifth member of the Politburo Standing Committee and the highest-ranked new entrant. Xi was clearly the favoured successor now.

Being the designated successor is a double-edged sword in modern Chinese politics. One issue is simply that there have never been clear rules about succession. Mao went through three successors, two of them meeting very sticky ends, before his final one, Hua Guofeng, succeeded in briefly replacing him. But how could anyone replace the irreplaceable?

By 1980 the position of Chairman of the Party, which Mao had occupied since the 1940s, was simply abolished. Hua rapidly faded into insignificance, eclipsed by the more experienced and formidable operator Deng. Deng himself fared little better in finding a worthy replacement, with another two falling by the wayside before finally, in Jiang Zemin, he found an unlikely but reliable Party leader. Between Jiang and Hu there was a relatively clean changeover – at least on the surface. But Jiang maintained active links to the Party's elite management, both formally and informally, well into Hu's decade in power. Some would argue he never stopped meddling. For Xi, therefore, the simple fact that he occupied prime position in 2007 meant little. The responsibilities he was given, too, were symbolically high, but nowhere near as demanding as those of the younger leader elevated along-side him, Li Keqiang. While Li had to deal with issues arising from intractable headaches like the management of welfare and health, Xi's main function was to chair the committee arranging the 2008 Olympics, head the Party School and busy himself with Party matters. The one conclusion he seems to have drawn from observing the very high failure rate of his predecessors in this dreaded 'favoured successor' slot was the importance of keeping a very low profile. Like Hu in the period from 1993 to 2002, he made a virtue of saying very little. Even his prolific blogging and writing ceased. The sole moment of indiscretion was during a visit to Mexico in 2009 when he was infamously caught on a microphone complaining about 'foreigners with full bellies pointing their fingers at China'. From 2012, this confident, push-ier attitude was to come increasingly to the fore. At the time, however, it was unclear whether this was a real insight into Xi's soul, or simply standard lines produced by grumpy, jet-lagged officials from the upper levels of the Party.

The period of transition in the elite leadership between 2011 and 2012 seems like ancient history from the vantage point of 2018. But the 18th Party Congress took place during a period of heightened sensitivity and drama, much of which was unintended. The most important event during this period was the death of Neil Heywood in a three-star hotel room in the south-western city province of Chongqing. Heywood, a British businessman, had been based in China since the 1990s, and his career had been closely linked with that of Bo Xilai, the ambitious, charismatic leader mentioned earlier. Bo was the son of a man called Bo Yibo, one of the 'Eight Immortals' who had been present since the inception of the Communist Party in China, who had died in 2005 aged almost 100. Although Bo, his wife Gu Kailai and son Bo Guagua seem to have been acquainted with Heywood, the links to the businessman's death were unclear. In 2011, the initial story had been that Heywood had simply drunk himself to death during a business trip to the city. But in February 2012, in extremely dramatic circumstances, Wang Lijun, Bo's chief security aide, fled to neighbouring Chengdu and took refuge in the American consulate there. Over the next few hours, he apparently divulged immense amounts of information, most of it implicating his erstwhile boss. Bo lasted until March but was then removed and his wife arrested, this time for Heywood's murder.

Skill might be important in politics, but luck is equally crucial. In ancient Rome, Cicero talked of the ways in which Fortuna swings backwards and forwards, bringing either good or bad fortune. The key thing is to grasp opportunity. We can only speculate now, but had Bo been able to maintain his career, and succeeded in being elevated to the Standing Committee, as had widely been expected before Heywood's demise, then he would have been a formidable opponent for Xi to face – and someone who would have proved challenging to rein in. It is generally unwise to subscribe to overheated conspiracy theories, but the categorical, quick removal of such a potential competitor was, for Xi, a pure gift. So too was the somewhat frenetic, jittery atmosphere this and other events of 2012 helped create. An already cautious group of leaders became even more so. This transition was important in creating a sense of stability for the Party. The fact that it had now attracted global interest only intensified the pressure.

The final surprise before the date of the 18th Party Congress, held later in the year, was Xi's disappearance in September during a visit to China by the then Secretary of State Hillary Clinton. Theories about why Xi had suddenly vanished ranged from an illness following a swimming accident to injuries he had allegedly sustained during an assassination attempt. Afterwards, a set of other causes were posited – that Xi had walked out angrily because of all the horse-trading about who might be promoted at the congress, and had made it clear to Jiang, Hu and other core decision makers that he was planning to walk out if they did not give him more support. To this day, no one knows quite what happened; the most we can say is that the whole atmosphere before mid-November in Beijing was clouded by intrigue, scheming and plots almost as thick as the smog that continued to smother the city. Right up to the congress itself, there was a lack of clarity about what might happen, who might appear in the final line-up of leaders, and how the order of proceedings might go. Matters were not helped by the congress lasting several days longer than had been expected. The final day, 15 November, saw the appearance of the new Standing Committee pushed back by almost an hour. When they finally appeared, reduced from nine to seven, the immediate impression was of a missed opportunity. Figures like Liu Yunshan and Zhang Dejiang seemed extremely conservative. More exciting Party members like Wang Yang had not been promoted. Sitting in a hotel lobby in Beijing at the time the new leadership emerged and watching proceedings on a television screen there, I, like many other commentators, felt it was a victory for cautiousness. But perhaps what we did not fully understand at that time was that it was not a leadership of equals, but one placed there to support and carry forward the programme of one man. And from

15 November, Xi Jinping would increasingly be seen as central to the new narrative the Party was promoting. We did not then appreciate it, but the era of Xi Jinping as the dominant leader had begun.

2

XI JINPING AS PARTY MAN

In the weeks before his final elevation in late 2012, Xi met with a famous liberal scholar, Hu Deping. During the discussion, Xi reportedly acknowledged the great challenges that China faced. The four 'uns' made famous by Wen Jiabao, former premier, a few years earlier, figured prominently. China was using an economic model that was unstable, unsustainable, unbalanced and inequitable. The 2008 global financial crisis had underlined this. China's economic model, mostly based on manufacturing, had been shown to be vulnerable to the vagaries of an outside world which had proved itself, once again, to be capricious and fickle. Already, fears of the dreaded middle-income trap were looming on the horizon: as the political scientist Minxin Pei put it, that the country might be trapped in a transition between being the world's factory and a place more reliant on services. China still had an economic model characterised by distortions: high levels of capital investment in fixed assets, low levels of consumption, a service sector that was growing but still lower than in other, similar, economies, and finally high, and unknown, amounts of public debt, particularly at local levels. To cap all this, no one knew the full situation as local officials had exaggerated in some areas while under-reporting in others, to protect their own backs. Statistics were therefore regarded with suspicion.

These distortions were accompanied by a population who had not experienced a recession since the time of Mao. Technically, in fact, the country's economy had not had a contraction for decades. Even when the Chairman had been steering the ship using his highly primitive, autarkic, centralised economic model there had been growth. Younger Chinese had always lived in a context of annual double-digit growth as normal, not an aberration. Since the mid-1990s, the middle classes – those living in urban centres, working in services and starting to enjoy the paraphernalia of the kinds of lifestyle experienced by similar socio-economic groups in the West – had moved from dreaming about having a freezer, a small scooter, a television and a phone to now wanting new, good-quality housing, a clean living environment, a car (usually imported, despite the huge tariffs), and the latest mobiles and electronic gadgets. For this demographic, their expectations and demands knew no bounds. Even more worryingly, they were increasingly aware of their new (albeit limited) legal rights, and were willing to protest, either through the courts or via petitions or other means, in order to be listened to.

All these issues must have been on Xi's mind when he met Hu in mid-2012. But there were also more explicitly political issues underlying their discussions. For instance, both men had a heightened awareness of how the one-party model had fared so badly in most other places, particularly in the Soviet Union, and there was also a sense that the Hu Jintao era had been about one story, and one alone – pumping out enormous amounts of growth at the expense of everything else. Since 2001, China had quadrupled the size of its economy. But it had also seen huge increases in inequality, with more billionaires than any other country but also 100 million people still living in poverty. The natural environment was at breaking point, with rapid industrialisation triggering extreme weather patterns and causing the ice caps on the Tibetan Plateau to melt. The worst environmental problem, politically, was the dense smog now descending across coastal China from Shanghai up to Beijing, which was having an impact on people's breathing, leading to premature deaths from bronchial problems, and generally advertising the limits of the government's powers to deliver the good lifestyle it had promised. Added to these issues were huge demographic challenges – an ageing population due to the one-child policy in place since the 1970s and 1980s, gender imbalances, and increases in the incidence of the sort of diseases that had blighted developed countries, such as cancer, heart disease and obesity. As some observers caustically put it, China was a country that was growing old before it got rich and poisoning itself before it became fully developed.

The lost years of Hu, as they came to be called, had gifted his successor with one massive asset – a truly vast economy, with plenty of room to grow. The issue was what to do about the country's political and administrative challenges. It would be impossible to continue pumping out massive amounts of growth; there would have to be a slowdown at some point. The issue then was about efficiency: China needed better management, not breakneck production of GDP. A leadership focused on political rather than economic issues was on the horizon. The question was what shape this politics would take, and how the new leaders would be able to utilise the immense benefits such a huge economy brought them. Broadly, the Party had a choice – either to consider fundamental reforms to the political realm before things got out of control, or to act counter-intuitively and have a period of retrenchment, devising a new form of reform and modernisation that would maintain political restraint and serve the one-party model but make it possible to navigate the difficult transition to middle-income status.

All this gives the context for Xi Jinping's first words on 15 November 2012, when he emerged as General Secretary of the Communist Party in Beijing after the tumultuous events of the previous few months. There were three salient points in his brief speech that day. The first was the way he stressed that the Party narrative was intrinsically part of a national one, with rejuvenation at its heart:

> Our responsibility is to unite and lead people of the entire Party and of all ethnic groups around the country while accepting the baton of history and continuing to work for realising the great revival of the Chinese nation in order to let the Chinese nation stand more firmly and powerfully among all nations around the world and make a greater contribution to mankind.

The second was to stress the notion of service – of the Party still abiding by the ethos from the earliest era of its existence of being a servant of the Chinese people:

> This great responsibility is the responsibility to the people [...] Our people love life and expect better education, more stable jobs, better income, more reliable social security, medical care of a higher standard, more comfortable living conditions, and a more beautiful environment.

The sense of the Party serving the expectations of the country's people was now set in a new context in which China had become wealthier, meaning expectations had increased. In the past, as leaders often said, the main objective had been for everyone to have food and clothing. Fulfilling these most basic needs was viewed as the construction of the primary stage of socialism. But now those elemental material needs had been met, there was a complex set of different demands, ranging from good healthcare to education provision, foreign travel, housing and a clean environment.

Thirdly, there was the issue of what the Party's function was in all of this. It was, as Xi made clear, a 'political' party:

> Our responsibility is to work with all comrades in the party to be resolute in ensuring that the Party supervises its own conduct; enforces strict discipline; effectively deals with the prominent issues within the Party; earnestly improves the Party's work style and maintains close ties with the people. So that our Party will always be the firm leadership core for advancing the cause of socialism with Chinese characteristics.

Even someone with no background in Chinese politics would be struck by how each of these three key points was focused on the Party, and on its centrality to the narrative of China's national development. It was clear from his speech that Xi was a Party man – and that his central mission was to ensure that its hold on power was sustainable. The key challenge was to convince the people that the Party did not want power for power's sake, but to advance a greater cause – that of national rejuvenation.

Since Xi Jinping took the helm in 2012, these three core themes have featured throughout the various actions, meetings and policy initiatives that the Party has pursued. A future story has been mapped out in which, using short- and longer-term goals as milestones, the Party takes the nation towards its moment of destiny. The most important landmarks in this future are referred to as the 'two centennial goals', the first of which will be in 2021 when China will achieve middle-income status and the CPC will celebrate its centenary. Under Hu, this was called the 'historic mission', a phrase that Xi returned to on 18 October 2017 in his report to the 19th Congress. That remains in hand. China now has a centrality in global issues as never before – from concerns about the environment to support for free trade, to its contribution to development through the Belt and Road Initiative (BRI). The country has finally been recognised externally as a global power, and I will deal with this issue in more detail later on.

Regarding the second point in Xi's inaugural speech, that of the importance of the Party's political function to serve the people, his priority has been to offer a clarification of the Communist Party's role in society and its core messages. These were spelled out in some detail in the recognition of Xi Jinping Thought and the language relating to the modernisation of socialism with Chinese characteristics which was written into the Party constitution in 2017. On the administrative side, the anti-corruption struggle, ongoing since 2013, has instilled discipline into the Party, and its role is now much more clearly political. It has aimed to create a space in society for other actors to work towards the main strategic goal it has stewardship over – delivering a rich, strong, powerful country.

Before we look in detail at the areas mentioned at the start of this chapter, we have to address the question of why the Party is so important to Xi's overall mission and his style of politics. This is a hugely important issue. The claim explored in the Introduction that Xi is a powerful leader – that he has more power than any of his predecessors and might even be as powerful, if not more so, than Mao – needs to be examined by considering what the Party is, and its relationship to him as its leader.

The Communist Party of China has been called resilient, adaptive, authoritarian, fragmented, Leninist and consultative. The adjectives mount up. If nothing else, they testify to how hard it has been to categorise the Party. Looking at its history, we can find some clues. The Party emerged from the broad efforts to modernise China during the twilight years of the Qing dynasty prior to 1911. Marx's ideas, via Japanese translations into Chinese, first found their way into the country in the first decade or so of the twentieth century, but they were simply part of a broad confluence of ideas and beliefs that intellectuals, many of whom had studied abroad, were using to get to grips with the immensely problematic question of why it was that China, with its rich history of early scientific achievement, had fallen so far behind. While Japan had steamed ahead, emerging from centuries of pre-modern isolation to embrace industrialisation, technology and modern governance, China had remained stuck in a largely agrarian or small artisan economy.

The tiny handful of early communists were nurtured, and in a sense grew up, in the shadow of the great 1917 revolution in Russia. When the USSR was finally established, and had some stability, it was able to send aid, personnel and inspiration to its comrades in China. Up to 1927, the Communist Party of China was almost wholly dependent on its Russian big brother. But a savage attack against it by the nationalists resulted in a rethink, largely led by Mao Zedong. Bit by bit, the Chinese found their own path, seeking support in rural areas, setting up the Red Army and articulating a more practical doctrine.

Under Mao the Party became nationalist and indigenised, with everything 'according to Chinese characteristics'. These are the two identities that have stuck, despite the radical shifts in its specific ideology and the economic programmes it has pursued. The overall vision has always been to use Marxism to fulfil the creation of a rich, strong, powerful Chinese nation. Mao's contribution to the Party as a revolutionary, guerrilla movement is well appreciated. But the shift from being a revolutionary party to one in government proved difficult. In many ways, its prime attribute under Mao was how it always seemed to be on a war footing, fighting against class enemies, enemies within and outside China, clashing with UN forces in the Korean peninsula, the Indians, the Russians and, finally, the Vietnamese in the years up to 1979. Internally and externally, Mao's China, infected by dialectics, was not a tranquil place.

The Party may have radically altered its approach to governance since the reform and opening-up period in 1978, but its overarching commitment to the creation of that great dream – a strong, powerful, confident China restored to its place at the centre of the region and the world – never once dimmed. For all the mistakes it made (and there were many, from the Great Leap Forward to the tragic famines of the early 1960s, and then the grotesque political pantomime of the Cultural Revolution for the decade from 1966), its underlying commitment to a powerful, strong country never wavered. Invoking this commitment remains the Party's chief rationale to this day, and it operates as a justification of every action the Party has ever undertaken.

For those unfamiliar with this grand nationalist commitment of the Party, making sense of the dramatic shifts, reverses and changes over the last seven decades proves bewildering. How can it be that a leader like Xi, living in the fourth decade of the Party under reform, can bridge the gap between pre- and post-1978 history, with its radical differences? Up until Mao's death, the economy had almost totally been in the hands of the state, in ways which were more extreme than they had ever been in the Soviet Union. There were no entrepreneurs, largely because they had all been thrown in jail. The chief ideological commitment was to strive for utopian goals through the cleansing of society, removing the class enemies in it. China supported revolutionary struggle abroad in such an idiosyncratic way that by 1967 it had only one ambassador serving overseas – Huang Hua, in Egypt. From 1978, albeit in controlled phases, all of this changed. The class struggle vanished, and a market economy arose under close state scrutiny. Entrepreneurs became increasingly important. China accepted foreign capital abroad, and, even more extraordinarily, started exporting money in the form of investments. By 2017, it was the chief trading partner for more than 120 countries.

Is it possible for these stories to belong to the same entity, or are they really two different ones? And is the party writing them actually a single coherent organisation, or in fact something resurrected, reformed and reborn after the Maoist onslaught of the 1960s? As the previous chapter showed, Xi himself has personal experience of this period and remembers it all too well. He has been called a Maoist, but that description would make no sense to him. Instead, he is the inheritor of a tradition in which Mao played a seminal role. There will be no de-Stalinisation in China. Mao will remain embalmed in his shrine/tomb in Tiananmen Square at the centre of the country. This is because Xi is the inheritor of the Party's commitment from its very beginnings to use whatever means necessary to ensure that China, with its searing history of suffering, victimisation and colonial bullying at the hands of outsiders, would never return to this state of vulnerability.

To truly understand why the Party gets its strength and legitimacy from this history, we need to recall just how horrifying life in China had been prior to communism. By the turn of the nineteenth century, China was entering a period of ominous stagnation and imminent decline which had begun during the period of high imperial culture of the mid-Qing dynasty, under the three great emperors Kangxi, Yongzheng and Qianlong, who had ruled, between them, for a total of 140 years. The clues to this decline were visible from within and outside – from China's capitulation to the British in 1842 following the first Opium War, to the horrifying casualties sustained during the Taiping Rebellion of 1850–64. The Beijing imperial court was riddled with factionalism, but largely held under the sway of conservatives. China gained the unenviable name of 'the sick man of Asia'. But for a culture with such strong pride and identity, and a powerful sense of its historic coherence, much worse lay in store. After the fall of the Qing in 1911, the Republic era intimated a new period of modernisation. But China's reward for fighting on the side of the Allies in World War I was to see the concessions held by the defeated Germany in its territory ceded to Japan. In the 1920s, the country was beset by regional divisions and imbalances. With the rise of militaristic leadership in Japan, China's vulnerability and its lack of any meaningful modern military, navy or infrastructure made it a prime target for annexation, and from 1932 the Japanese mounted a series of provocations and attacks, resulting in all-out war from 1937.

The issue of the Sino-Japanese War is by no means finished for Xi Jinping and his comrades, even though they are the first generation of elite leaders born after 1949. Lived memory of the epic war fades by the year, but its commemoration is a heavy burden to shoulder, one which every leader needs to address. The matter is complicated by China's historically contentious relationship with Japan, which reaches back not decades or centuries but millennia. This relationship is characterised by competitiveness and deep resentment, and the 1937 war was the most savage manifestation of this. In China's view, tensions have been exacerbated by the failure of the Japanese to fully accept their culpability in the same manner as the Germans did in Europe after 1945.

The Communist Party is a product of this history, and is infused with the country's particular need for moral retribution and delivery of justice for its people. That, more than anything else, remains the Party's most powerful source of appeal. And while its tactics since 1978 have been to use economic means to deliver power, the end product is the same – a unified, stable China able to relate to and deal with the world on its own terms. A China, as late Nobel laureate Liu Xiaobo put it, returned to its place at the centre of the world.

Xi did not construct this historical narrative; he simply occupies a place within it. He is the current lead in the story, but he did not write the words, or even decide when the final act might be. Like any actor, therefore, his real skill is in his performance rather than the creation of a whole new work off his own back. In this context, the elite leadership of the Party resembles a five-act play, with Mao in the first, Deng in the second, Jiang and Hu in the third and fourth respectively, and Xi now central to the final act. His responsibility is to make sure that we are not watching a tragedy but a stirring drama of moral resurrection and restoration of justice to the Chinese people. They are the true masters of this drama, and it is on their behalf that the Party is performing.

Despite his current pre-eminence, Xi Jinping remains a product of a Party training process which has produced many tens of thousands of other leaders. The only option for these people to wield power in Chinese politics, albeit in an organised context, is within the Party. There are no other options in the political arena. And that has involved the acceptance of a specific culture, ideology and world view, service to which remains critical. For those who progress to leadership, a very specific tone and space to operate within is already set. It means belonging to an elite cadre who function as servants of the great meta-narrative – a unified Party bringing about a rejuvenation of a great nation, using the tools of Marxism–Leninism and Mao Zedong Thought. The latter is simply the 'Sinification' of the former: an application of the universal principles of dialectic materialism to build the appropriate societal superstructure, but always – and this is the crucial addition – in ways which are in accordance with the specific situation in China and Chinese national conditions.

China, the USSR and other communist one-party systems have frequently used the promotion of a cult of personality and the creation of a charismatic leader as a strategic tool to communicate their ideology to people and to mobilise them. The extensive use of propaganda featuring Mao and the levels of adoration surrounding him were phenomenal during the Cultural Revolution, meaning that in some sense this era is the only one in Chinese history where there was a universal belief system linked to the spiritual attributes of one superhuman figure. Under subsequent leaders, there have been high levels of resistance to this worship of a single leader. But that does not remove the importance of promoting leaders' individual personalities and stories. The leader is a powerful strategic tool, acting as a moral exemplar and demonstrating the Party's ideological commitment, unity and cohesiveness. The leader's individual qualities are part of its identity and crucial to the way it operates.

Does this mean that Xi Jinping is the new Mao, as has often been claimed?

The best way to answer that question is to look at context. The China of Mao was a radically different place to that which exists today, one in which the media, industry and political messages were accessible only to regimes of control. During the Mao era the country was isolated, its borders tightly closed, its newspapers, radio stations and few television outlets under centralised management structures. Most people lived in rural areas, where the Party was the only viable organising entity. The China of Xi Jinping, on the other hand, saw 120 million people travel outside the country's physical borders in 2015 alone. China is now a place where more than 50 per cent of economic activity is in the hands of non-state organisations. It is a place where 3 million young people have studied abroad since 1980, and where over 200 million are learning English. Almost a billion Chinese people now have mobile phones, and through these access to the internet, albeit one guarded by the Great Firewall. Even with these restrictions, these Chinese have access to freedoms and are able to make life choices that would have been unimaginable to their forebears under Mao. Calling Xi Jinping the Mao of modern China is as meaningful as calling Donald Trump the George Washington of the US. The times they live in are too radically different for the comparison to make any sense.

Even more striking is that unlike Mao, Xi is a Party man through and through. Mao was famously able to defy and challenge the Communist Party during the Cultural Revolution by accusing it of becoming ossified by bureaucracy and self-interest, threatening in the mid-1960s to resign from the Party and retreat to the countryside to raise a new force to seize power. This was no idle threat: his charismatic hold over the Chinese people was so powerful that few doubted his ability to do this. Xi, on the other hand, would never make such a threat. He is powerful because the Party he leads is powerful, and he has no individual power outside of that structure and context.

Xi's role as a Party man gives meaning to his main actions since coming to power in 2012. Unlike his predecessor, his leadership has been political, rather than administrative or economic. Whereas under Hu the country's focus was on GDP growth and pumping out new economic results, Xi has been working to consolidate the role of the Party in its national mission to make the country strong and great. He has sponsored Party-led building campaigns, promoted the Party line and enforced ideology and discipline, the last of these as part of the national struggle against corruption. All his tasks as leader have been completely focused on the

Party and its health, sustainability and centrality. With this in mind, it is clear why Xi was so keen to underline the importance of the Party's role in his November 2012 speech. It is an absolutely central and integral part of his leadership.

3

XI JINPING'S VALUES?

The concept of Xi Jinping Thought is an anomaly. When they first arrive in the great city of Shanghai, visitors gaze from the Bund across to the skyscrapers ranged along the other side of the Huangpu River and wonder how a communist country regarded as the archetypal enemy by the West during most of the Cold War era now looks like any other thriving capitalist global centre. They will see few or no clues that the Communist Party still exercises a monopoly over the landscape in front of them. If they look very, very closely, they might spot the odd hammer and sickle, or see the occasional slogan plastered across a public wall. But even these do not feel overtly political any more.

The idea that communist ideology still matters in today's China is a hard concept to grasp. Surely if there is any ideology at all it must be capitalism based mostly on the Western model, though without the political order that prevails there. And yet despite this vibrant, marketised environment that exists throughout China, communist ideas have made a comeback under Xi. There is much more focus on the cadres in the Party learning about new developments in Marxism–Leninism. Party-building has become a priority. Party schools, from the central one in Beijing (known in full as the Party School of the Central Committee of the Communist Party of China, or the Central Party School) down to Pudong in Shanghai, Jinggangshan in Jiangxi, and elsewhere across the country, run packed programmes conveying the latest ideological messages. For a country that is often dismissed as pursuing hard, pragmatic aims and merely playing lip service to the old Marxist tropes, this seems an enormous amount of effort to expend on something that is apparently of little importance.

Even more extraordinary is the amount of time and effort that elite leaders like Xi have put into promoting these ideas and coming up with new ideological terms. With so many more pressing problems, it seems odd to people outside China that he used so much political capital on getting Xi Jinping Thought into the Party constitution during the October 2017 congress. And why has this seemingly archaic concept been regarded as so important?

In essence, the reason for the importance of Xi Jinping Thought is this: in China, an extremely complex and potentially fragmented country, this ideological consensus has been hard won, and once agreement is reached, it must be well defended. Getting agreement on a single belief system for the political elite is not the business of a day, or even a year. It takes decades, and the expenditure of much blood, sweat and tears. Having a broad consensus among the main leaders of the Communist Party and the Party state under it means that they have a common language. It might be a language that only they care about and understand. But – at least for them – it works, much as medieval Latin created a common language across a fragmented Europe for members of an elite who would have otherwise been unable to speak to each other easily. Do most Chinese people now believe in Marxism–Leninism? Almost certainly not. But they accept that their political leaders stand by this belief system, and as long as they get the strong, rich country and the material prosperity that flows from this, then they tolerate the Party's eccentric belief system.

It is harder to grapple with the question of whether a leader like Xi Jinping believes in Marxism–Leninism in his heart of hearts. Leaders before him, such as Deng Xiaoping, were almost blasé in their dismissal of too much book study of ideology. For them, it was more a question of adopting some basic tenets and then putting them into practice. In that sense, it was almost like a religious practice, a belief system that spoke to people's emotional and rational side and supplied a framework for change, engagement and action. For later leaders like Xi, we must also consider whether they have had any real choice over the belief system they have inherited. As stated earlier, Xi applied to join the Communist Party many times in the early 1970s before eventually getting in. This was not necessarily a sign of fervent belief in its ideology, then, but more a reflection of the fact that membership supplied at least some security and a future at a time when these things were in short supply. Joining the Party was the only choice; therefore, in that sense, it was no choice at all. Party members who developed careers over the following decades never had to make major decisions about their political orientation. They were Party members, and accepting its ideology was just a part of their responsibilities. There were no rewards for pondering its ultimate justification or the soundness of its principles. There have been very few times in the country's recent history when the Party's beliefs have been questioned, and when fierce debates took place in the 1980s about the role of the market, which involved some question of choice, Xi had not yet been senior enough to get involved. Even then, the argument had been in the context of modifying Party ideology, rather than resisting or opposing it. For Xi, therefore, it has largely been a question of accepting this ideology, with innovation only permitted when absolutely necessary, and only under tight constraints. The one given, however, is that for the Party – for its culture and identity and way of operating – that ideology has to be present. Xi Jinping, therefore, believes in ideology and its value, but would probably not pass the kind of intermediate exam on elements of Marxism–Leninism that is sometimes set at Party schools or in universities. This should not surprise us. Theresa May, the British prime minister at the time of writing, would be unlikely to be able to write much about classical conservative philosophy from the time of Burke. Countries' leaders are practitioners. They do, and others think.

For someone who has put so much emphasis on the importance of the Party, of restoring its moral status and its political function in society, ideology for Xi has great functional importance. It is a tool to create the all-important sense of unity and purpose. It sits at the heart of the identities of the 88 million members of the Party – whatever else they are or may be, they all at least believe they should believe in something – and they are told what to believe in. Being faithful followers, once these edicts are issued they don't argue with them.

At the end of 2017, on paper at least, the Communist Party of China believes in Mao Zedong Thought, Deng Xiaoping Theory, the Three Represents, Scientific Development and Xi Jinping Thought. This is a complex menu to carry around in one's head. Mao Zedong Thought is relatively easy to describe – the 'Sinification' of Marxism so that it accords to Chinese national characteristics. Deng Xiaoping Theory is the adoption of market socialism, basically the acceptance of a more pragmatic form of Marxism–Leninism. The Three Represents and Scientific Development are simple developments from

Deng's time. The first allowed entrepreneurs from the non-state sector to enter the Party, while the second aimed for a more balanced, people-centred growth rate. Xi Jinping Thought occupies a space somewhere in the great Chinese communist ideological tradition that is based on these core thoughts. What might Xi Jinping Thought be, however?

For the answer, we have to look at the development of Party ideology since 2012. The first sign of what Xi might want to promote came with the 'China Dream' language of 2013. Tied into already extant ideas about the country being on a historic mission towards regeneration and a Chinese renaissance, the China Dream brought these down to the level of people's daily aspirations. For them, the notion was simple but very powerful: to have the same standard of life, welfare and opportunities as people in developed countries. The millions of Chinese who travelled abroad in 2013 had the opportunity to see first-hand the housing, cities, environments and lifestyles of people in places like Australia, America and Europe. For many of these travellers, their wealth levels were already comparable to the people in these countries. They wanted to *have* the good life – not simply the promise of one, as their parents and grandparents had had. They wanted good-quality cars and food, and the best education for their children. At its heart, the China Dream recognised that the Communist Party was building a bourgeois China – a place where the middle classes were king, both as consumers and workers, and a source of both potential tax revenue as a result of their higher wages and new growth through spending, rather than manufacturing and investment. This group, estimated to range from around half a billion up to three-quarters of a billion people, was Xi's core audience, the one that he and his government had to speak to, appeal to the aspirations of and remain relevant to. The Party needed to dream their dream with them, and *for* them. It could not lose this group. It if did, it would lose everything.

In October 2013, a plenum was held, with great fanfare, to add more content to this idea. The third plenum of the 11th Congress, which had taken place in December 1978, had previously marked the moment of reforms to be carried out over the following four decades, and there was a sense of expectation that the 2013 plenum would be a similar historic turning point. More reforms were needed. State enterprises remained poor in terms of profitability and productivity. Growth was slowing down, falling from double digits in 2010 to just under 7 per cent. China seemed to be afflicted with what some called a looming 'middle-income trap' – the country was no longer a cheap place to manufacture goods because of rising costs and wages, but it was still not a fully developed service economy either. To avoid this, it needed to enter a new period of radical reorientation where it could address some of its most pressing challenges, the impediments to achieving its dream – the poor environment, inequalities in society, high levels of debt. The list went on. Under Xi, now was the moment to enter with energy into a new era of reform.

Everyone loves the word 'reform' in China. It has given its name to the era since 1978. Reform is regarded as an unmitigated good. In a sense this captures the complex situation that China finds itself in – the country has been in a perpetual state of dissatisfaction for the last four decades, and has used this as a means of getting ahead. Reform has been the fuel that has fired this immense age of aspiration and ambition. And the Party, with its propaganda, narratives and messaging, has managed – so far – to capture this.

At the heart of reform in China, however, there has always been the challenge of needing to square a circle by managing tensions between the state and the market, whose relationship is usually confrontational. The state restrains, the market liberates. The state represents prescription, rules, constraints, burdens and limits. In the Hobbesian view it is there to prevent evil, not to do good. The market is its polar opposite – it represents liberty, energy, freedom, dynamism and giving people their own individual space where they are free to do whatever business they want, buy what they want, earn what they want. There are no limits beyond those set by logic and the state. For believers in the free market, the key aim is to ensure that the state is pushed further and further away, until it as good as disappears.

The more leftist leaders in the 1980s resisted the idea of marketisation, sometimes fiercely. People like Deng Liqun (no relative of Deng Xiaoping) and Chen Yun accepted the notion of a market – but only within the parameters of a socialist state where it performed specific functions and needed constant policing and political ordering. With its experimentation and liberalism, the 1980s often became like a game of cat and mouse, with the space in which entrepreneurs worked largely unregulated. Sometimes these entrepreneurs were accepted by the state, other times they were thrown in jail. One well-known example is the founder of the famous Shazi ('Fools') sunflower seeds brand, a feisty farmer called Nian Guangjiu, who had been in and out of jail during the Maoist era and then come into his own in the Deng period. Pulled before a judge in the mid-1980s for yet more claims of embezzlement and corruption, when charged with having had several lovers he fiercely protested, shouting at the judge that there had been at least two dozen!

This issue of the market's role within China was no laughing matter, however. The student uprising in 1989 nearly felled the Party, with hardliners on the more statist side claiming victory and pointing out the perils of allowing too much space to non-state actors and forces that the Party simply could not control. The octogenarian Deng's response to this was his 1991–2 Southern Tour, where he made a new commitment to continuing reform and using the market to deliver material prosperity to the people. This, after all, was allowed under the crucial iteration of 'socialism with Chinese characteristics'. It didn't matter that no one else had yet managed to combine market-isation with a one-party system. The collapse of the Soviet Union in 1991 was another fillip to the conservatives, though, who argued fiercely that the same fate would await China if it did not maintain tight political control. Broadly, this combined approach has been the default in the era from Jiang onwards: the Party has been walking a tightrope between marketisation, which has involved more and more reform of state-run enterprises and the central state retreating from areas in which it had once been all-powerful, and aggressive preservation of the privileged space that the Party still needs to control, such as organised political activity and political stewardship of the main state enterprises in key sectors – telecoms, energy and finance in particular.

The 2013 plenum decision therefore was another stage of this grand, decades-old argument. It was the first time that the Party had stated that the market was necessary for reform. Before this, the market had been referred to as useful, preferential or simply a part of reform, all of which were weaker formulations. To say that it was necessary was a much stronger statement. For all the excitement of this announcement, however, it was soon tempered by the equally adamant line on the next page – that the state should play a commanding role in the economy. The cage of state control within which the bird of the market flew, as the 1980s phrase in China put it, was still there, but it had grown a bit larger, and a bit less visible.

Another striking thing about the 2013 plenum communiqué was that it contained 60 policy initiatives, covering areas from the economy (promising hybrid ownership of state enterprises), to the environment (promising clean skies and water, and safe food), to fiscal administration (more powers devolved to the provinces). This was supplemented by a personal explanatory statement from Xi himself, which set out the rationale behind the raft of new reforms. Standing back from this tsunami of initiatives and promises, the immediate impression was that of ambition, and of comprehensiveness.

'Comprehensiveness' was an oft-used keyword, which featured in a Party slogan formalised in 2016 – the 'Four Comprehensives'. These were:

- **TO COMPREHENSIVELY BUILD A MODERATELY PROSPEROUS SOCIETY:** The idea that China was aiming to be a middle-income country by 2021 was first mooted in the Hu era. Under Xi, 2021 has figured as the first of two centennial goals, this one marking the foundation of the Communist Party in Shanghai in 1921. For an organisation that loves to celebrate an anniversary, the upcoming date marks an enormous symbolic moment. The 'moderately prosperous' moniker is a delightful piece of Party litotes. It would be more accurately expressed by 'semi-developed', because the meaning is easy to explain – a country which had a per capita GDP in 1978 of US$ 300 is, in 2021, looking to deliver a figure of around US$ 13,000. That raises it to the same category as countries like Russia, at least in per capita terms; in aggregate, China is a far larger economy. But middle-income status is also problematic. Development of this level of GDP elsewhere has usually involved what the Party fears most of all – political reform, with the new bourgeoisie wanting to participate in decision making, and this has often led to high levels of turbulence and contention in society. For the Party, whose role is to manage risk as much as everything else due to China's phenomenally complex economy, a transition which involves not just economic issues but also political ones is full of treacherous unknowns, threats and challenges. Prosperity involves stability, and the preservation of public peace and security. This, the First Comprehensive in the Xi ideology, therefore stresses a point of consensus – that the Party's function is to bring about the great, stable, prosperous nation, one guided by socialist equity and notions of justice and balance. That is the vision, in any case.

• **TO COMPREHENSIVELY DEEPEN REFORM:** 'Reform', as we have heard, is a good word. But there are as many types of reform as there are different crystal formations in snow. People want reform, but they do not know what kind of reform might work best. And Xi Jinping, for all the talk of his bold, charismatic leadership, is also from a leadership culture that is deeply conservative. Broadly, he works within the framework inherited from the one truly great reformer of the Chinese system in the last half a century – Deng Xiaoping. When Xi's position is placed alongside Deng's, immense differences can be seen. The reforms that Deng sat at the centre of wholly reformulated the nature of the state in China, allowing spaces to be opened up that had never been liberated before. Deng's reformist agenda allowed foreign capital, entrepreneurialism, the creation of a national science and technology sector (using high levels of training and education), and marketisation across almost every area of the economy.

Xi's ideas have not contested any of Deng's changes, although they have attempted to build on and develop them. In the social sphere, the one-child policy has been relaxed (some argue that it was never really a policy in the first place), with people now able to have two children. Take-up, however, has been tepid because of the immense costs of raising a child. The household registration system has also undergone incremental reform, so that those who originally held rural documents can now have proper status in cities, under certain conditions. Again, though, there have been issues with people wishing to maintain the land rights their old status gave them and being reluctant to relinquish their rural links. And some new fiscal powers have been granted to the provinces and sub-provincial levels of government. But on a host of other issues – from further reforms of the state sector, to taxation, to real devolution of powers from the centre – there has been little movement. And on the most important area of reform, that of political reform, there has been almost nothing. Many would even argue that things have moved backwards in this respect. In many ways, the most striking feature of the Xi era up to 2017 is the mismatch between the noisy rhetoric about reform and the lack of real efforts to put it into action. The Deng paradigm remains in place, uncontested. As far as reform goes, Xi Jinping Thought is at most an affirmation or a recommitment to change, but not an innovation. Nor has it remotely shaped a new paradigm for how to do things in China.

- **TO COMPREHENSIVELY GOVERN THE NATION ACCORDING TO LAW:** China as it has grown rich has shifted from what was called in the Maoist era 'Rule by man' to 'Rule of law'. The 'of' is important. The Chinese have made huge progress since 1979 in creating, almost from scratch, a legal system. In 2014 a whole plenum was devoted to it. Law, like reform, is a good word. And yet it does not involve copying the Western notion of 'rule by law'. There is 'rule by the Party', and no room for any competitors. So the solution under Xi is simply 'rule of law under the rule of the Party'. Building the infrastructure for this kind of circumscribed legality has been the focus of a lot of effort throughout the Xi era.

And implementation of the rules that exist has been improved. In the past, while China had well-written laws based on the continental system rather than on British common law, they were largely unheeded. Even the 1982 State Constitution was nicknamed 'Sleeping Beauty' because of its excellent-sounding content and poor value in defending anyone in court. Political interference in cases became a given, especially those which involved dissidents, national security or high-profile commercial issues. Under Xi, the focus has been to give a better deal to the all-important middle class, making it clear the government is on their side. For them, better property rights and more certainty and predictability when they experience commercial problems and seek legal recourse are tangible signs on their side. And in the last 30 years, Chinese people have become increasingly conscious of their rights and aware of their new powers, despite some narratives abroad stating that the country remains a bastion of repression and fear. Beyond the political sphere, on the whole the Chinese are perfectly willing, and ready, to energetically promote their interests. Business is booming for lawyers in the commercial sector. The 2014 reforms therefore shadowed the term 'market with Chinese characteristics', creating 'legality with Chinese characteristics'. Court administration was reformed, with funding clarified so that lower-level courts got their support from higher up rather than from the governments of the prefectures in which they were located. More training and professional development was promised for judges. And new laws were to be issued only after clear consultation, with the promise that where judgements were given there would be better implementation of these, and that officials would be expected to listen. On the ground, this reform seemed to have had an impact. Speaking to a local commercial lawyer in Inner Mongolia in 2016, I was told that for the first time local government officials were listening hard to what the courts said and doing what they ordered. On the delicate question of whether a court would ever be able to challenge the Party state on any important issues, however, the answer was also equally clear. This would not happen, and I will examine the topic further below.

TO COMPREHENSIVELY GOVERN THE PARTY: Party governance has always been a tricky issue. How could the Party make demands of society and take any kind of leadership role if it was part of the problem itself? During the Mao era, there had been no proper guidance or rules. The Party had been as much his victims as the people, and after surviving the Cultural Revolution it had, under Deng, set in place institutional safeguards. These included the introduction of unwritten time limits on terms of power, age limits that forced cadres to move on once they reached a certain age, and observance of the limits of governance by regularly holding congresses and ensuring a turnover of elite leaders. Succession, as Xi's case proved, was always a problem, but on the whole the Party became more self-regulated after 1978. In the era of Hu Jintao, the thorny issue of democratisation was sidestepped by talking of intra-Party democracy, with an increase in governance within the Party itself. But this did not seem to improve cadres' behaviour. Corruption, poor conduct and officials' impunity only seemed to worsen as the country became more wealthy.

Now, the abstractions of Hu's notion have largely been swept away by a more old-fashioned suite of actions under Xi. Effort has gone into the Maoist interdiction to focus on the practicalities of Marxism–Leninism in its 'Sinified' version. Observing the mass line, an idea that arose from the creation of the United Front just before the communists' victory in 1949, means that most of the effort is now expended on co-opting and unifying everyone under a new form of obedience, some of it involving clear coercion. Party-building and loyalty have been key. Even those under the highly unwelcome spotlight of the graft-busters, the Central Commission for Discipline Inspection, have been instructed to produce paeans of praise for the Party and Xi's leadership before their defenestration. Ling Jihua, former right-hand man of Hu Jintao and Politburo member from 2012, was unceremoniously removed for corruption in 2015 despite writing a stirring anthem of loyalty that was published in the Party's theoretical magazine, *Seeking Truth*, only months before his removal. Party-building became one of the key new responsibilities, with new ideological messages intensively produced and promoted – such as the Four Comprehensives outlined here – and training at Party schools entering a boom period. Xi himself undertook campaigns where he promoted the importance of Party discipline, speaking to the army, universities and the media, telling state-run China Central Television in early 2016 that they needed to act with 'responsibility'. The Party under Xi has cast off the shadow of factionalism and become more unified. Signs of dissent have been limited, despite the removal of many powerful figures during the anti-corruption struggle. A letter allegedly written by some figures in the Party surfaced in 2016, complaining about Xi's emerging cult of personality and annexation of power. But the mystery is not the appearance of such criticisms – it is more about their relative absence. Deng had to deal with powerful opposition throughout the early era of reform from figures such as Deng Liqun. Jiang Zemin had the formidable Zhu Rongji at his side, a person who attracted as much, if not more, respect. Hu Jintao always had to work in a world where Jiang or his protégés, despite having ostensibly retired, remained extremely active – and obstructive. Xi has been able to operate largely alone, on his own terms. This is curious in view of the huge challenges the Party is still facing, and the effort put into institutionalising its power over the last few years. The question here, therefore, is how can a leader seen by many outside China (and some – albeit very quietly expressed – within) as autocratic and imperious place something seemingly inimical to this sort of autocratic behaviour in his most exhaustively promoted ideological formulation? In essence, are the Four Comprehensives simply rhetoric, or a smokescreen while other things take place behind the scenes?

It was telling in itself that the Party was willing to declare it had a 'comprehensive plan'. Surely the day of complete state control of society and the economy is over. China is such a complex place, with massive differences between coastal and central areas and the western regions. With similar disparities between social groups in these areas, how could any overarching narrative possibly knit everything together in a way that would work for everyone? This is one of the most puzzling things about the Xi era. Never before has China contained more diversity in itself. Never before has it seemed more hybrid, both interlinked with the rest of the world and at the same time more segmented than ever between its different and often contrasting elements. And never before has it been harder to pin down any sort of commonality across all this diversity, except that it happens in a specific geography which goes under the name of 'China'. As one commentator wearily told me some years ago, 'China is not a country – it is a universe.' It obeys different rules and edicts – or likes to think it does.

Xi's strategy is to accept that there is a space outside the Party that it can no longer control – space that its own policies have allowed and which now must continue to exist. Ironically, with China's growth so dependent on the non-state sector, it is the Party which has become a parasite, relying on it to survive. The Party needs this sector to employ people and to deliver innovation and growth. It is also reliant on non-state actors to look after the elderly, the poor, the disenfranchised and the sick; it has made some space for civil society because it has had to. The state can no longer involve itself in every area of a person's life, as it once did. For a start, it doesn't have the resources. Every day since 1978, the Party has ceded space to other forces in society. Until Xi took the helm, it almost seemed to have become just one of several competing forces, sometimes almost begging for people's attention as they merrily went on their way, making money, living their lives, forging their ways in a world in which they almost never came across the Party.

With Xi's renewed focus on building the Party, and his emphasis on it having a clear role in society and well-defined boundaries in which to work, he has also re-energised the notion that it has a meaningful grand plan that stretches across society – a vision, as it were, that speaks to and relates to everyone. At the heart of this vision is the mission he referred to in his speech at the 19th Party Congress (discussed in the Introduction): to create a rejuvenated, powerful, rich country. According to the once-popular slogan 'No Communist Party of China, No New China', the Party was once the country's saviour. But now China is mobilised by nationalism, the love of country, the strong identity imputed to it and the feeling by most Chinese that their country is finally winning the battle to modernise, and will soon be restored to its rightful place at the centre of the world. When the Party speaks of these things, it taps into profound populism and gets public support. All past sins are forgotten. Now, the Party is the parasite of this sense of nationalism – with the argument implicit in much of what Xi and his fellow leaders say that without the stability, unity and strategic purpose which the Party provides, national resurrection will not happen. This is the new 'legitimising deal' the Party seeks; it derives its legitimacy from its nationalist credentials. The era of simply appealing to wealth creation is coming to an end, and after 2020 there will be no politically mandated GDP growth targets; the purpose of that era – to create a mountain of material wealth that China might use, under the leadership of the Party, to create a sustainable, globally respected, powerful country that will never again be a victim to outside aggression or its own internal fractures – has been achieved. From this point of view, it makes sense to have a comprehensive plan that is owned, directed and shaped by the Party. There is a plan with a clear outcome, and everyone is being driven towards this.

Under Xi, the Party has therefore created a more complex set of messages to accompany the ones about reform and opening up. These are manifested in the 'core socialist values' – a set of 24 characters that have appeared on hoardings at the side of roads, in newspapers, in Party literature and even in advertisements. These values are about justice, patriotism, legality, harmony, democracy and civility. They are about a society which is undergoing not just material change, but also fundamental moral, cultural and psychological transformations. Xi's China is the first time in the country's history where more people live in cities than in rural areas. It is one where most Chinese will live to be older than 75, where they have opportunities to travel, study and work globally in ways that would have been fantasies for the generations before them. But it is also the first time that the elderly outnumber the young, and where most people have no brothers or sisters because they were born in the era of the one-child policy. Such a China is different in almost every respect to those Chinas that have existed before. The Party's focus on promoting specific messages about ethics, public behaviour and notions of fair play is perhaps an admission not of its strengths but of the fact that it is the only entity that can do this – the one institution that stretches across the country and has the kind of reach that, for instance, a religious organisation might have in the West. Under Xi, the Party has had to speak not just about growth and productivity targets, but also about how people in this transformed, daily changing country need to treat each other, exist alongside each other and work with each other. It has become an entity which does not just support material growth, but also moral development and sustainability. Its 'core socialist values' have been the means to achieve this.

All this has necessitated the Party undergoing its own form of 'cultural revolution'. It has had to start looking like it actually believes in the values it had largely consigned to the realm of rhetoric in the past. In charge of such a momentous project to make China great – not again, but for the first time in modern history – it cannot allow itself to be distracted by diversions like creating wealth for its members rather than the whole of society, or simply existing for power's sake, rather than using this power to fulfil some aim. The aim is simple: national renaissance and rejuvenation. And the function of cadres is to shift their eyes away from the immediate inducements they are faced with and towards this great goal; they have to be disciplined, loyal to the message, obedient to the unity of the Party and completely committed. The anti-corruption struggle which began in 2013 has been the tactic used to achieve this. As the great ancient military strategist Sun Zi stated in his *Art of War*, tactics make no sense without strategy, and strategy cannot be delivered without tactics. Cleansing the Party core, making sure cadres are fit soldiers for undertaking this great task, is critically important. Without their complete obedience to the larger task of national rejuvenation, the whole project would be jeopardised. It might not even come about at all.

The anti-corruption struggle has been described as a power struggle, almost akin to that in the television series *House of Cards*, a description which Xi Jinping referred to when visiting the US in 2015. However, he said there was no reality in such a claim. The aim of the struggle has not been for him to accrue more personal power; the Party simply needed to deal with the issue of political inefficiency. In the fat years under Hu Jintao, where growth was plentiful and the Party almost like King Midas, turning everything it touched to gold, things could be lax. Party officials could occupy the shadowy realm between commerce and politics, never really aware of any boundary, allowing their networks to accrue wealth. A relationship, through patronage, family ties or even something more remote like a friend of a friend, was a market commodity which could be given a value in dollars. Being associated with a provincial official who might have decision-making powers over multimillion-dollar infrastructure or construction projects was worth a lot. Access to the summit of power in Beijing, the Standing Committee of the Politburo, was like gold dust – something that could be converted into multibillion-dollar returns. The closest kith and kin of top leaders were, if they wished (and most did), able to enjoy vast wealth-making opportunities because of the monetary value of these linkages. The main issue under Hu became not whether someone close to a top leader was on the make, but what possible reason there might be for someone *not* to be exploiting these opportunities. The clean ones were the people acting suspiciously, not the other way around.

Such shared collusion meant that once Xi started to move forward with his anti-corruption mission, he was faced with almost limitless targets. Everyone was potentially vulnerable. But it was about much more than being able to pick off people who might have been construed as his opponents or enemies. In a way, the manner in which he has constructed his political programme means that in contemporary China it is almost impossible to go against him. He is the master of the great narrative – to make China strong and powerful. Who would oppose that? The only issue is how best to ensure this happens. And an opponent would also be on shaky ground if they questioned whether the Party was fulfilling its main function, that of politics. If it wasn't, what would be its purpose? Therefore, the rationale for the struggle against malfeasance did not come from Xi alone; it was based on the simple logic that the Party, whose key asset had been its economic stewardship of state enterprises and which was now in charge of a country with falling growth and shrinking profits from these enterprises, could no longer allow parasites around top leaders to slope away with massive amounts of off-the-books assets. That was stealing from the Party, the state and the great vision itself – national regeneration. The people indulging in this behaviour were not just criminals. They were traitors.

The anti-corruption struggle developed into a movement which was as much about symbolism and the management of public perceptions as it was about trying to do anything long-term about cadre misbehaviour. High-profile targets like Zhou Yongkang fell from grace – the first time since 1949 that a former member of the Standing Committee had been hauled through an investigation and then punished in the civil courts. He was soon joined by Ling Jihua (mentioned earlier in this chapter), a member of the full Politburo. The notion of 'tigers and flies' being felled was important – no one was immune. Had every person who was guilty of some level of corruption been punished, however, the whole system would have collapsed. Instead, the arbitrary clampdowns on particular figures led to restraint and cautiousness and encouraged self-regulation by officials. They began to prevent their contacts from enriching themselves, rather than simply playing the game of the past – paying lip service to the rules while plundering in their daily lives. This was backed up by a new form of puritanism: limitations on travel and entertainment were so well implemented that luxury hotels saw a collapse in their profits and imports of expensive brands started to dwindle. All of that played well with the public, who were glad to see overmighty, pampered officials being disciplined for once.

From its beginnings in 2013 up until the retirement of the formidable Wang Qishan, who headed the Central Commission on Discipline and Inspection in 2017, the outcomes of the anti-corruption process have been mixed. After a period of confusion and meandering, the Party has reverted to a more traditional Leninist model, with a tightly disciplined, uniformed cadre elite who are in charge of the political direction of society and who ostensibly share a strong common ethos and vision. Unlike in the past, they keep their distance from moneymaking. They almost seem to live tough, self-sacrificing lives now, just as they did in the early Mao era when the Party had a much stronger moral standing. Party officials serve the people. (This spirit is exemplified in the figure of Lei Feng, a model soldier and Party member who lived every moment of his short life for the sake of others – or so the stories go – before being run over in the early 1960s by a reversing truck.) But they do so in a social context utterly different from the one that existed in the past. In society, dynamic economic changes, individualism, creation of personal networks through social media, and apolitical activity are what mark the lives of those outside the realm of Party leadership. These people are encouraged to do what they can to create wealth for

China and make money for themselves. They can become millionaires, even billionaires, and own as many cars and luxurious items as they can legally buy. As long as they do their business within the parameters of the law, newly refined and clarified, they can live the China Dream. And by living the China Dream, they are contributing to it.

The only problem now is that the envious officials looking at them, officials these wealthy Chinese would once have been passing large inducements and kickbacks to, are probably building up a deal of resentment within themselves. Being a cadre in modern China is increasingly like being a celibate priest in a society undergoing a rapid process of sexual liberalisation. Metaphorically speaking, how many can truly forgo the pleasures of the flesh when they are so ubiquitous? There is a real question about the sustainability of this posture – one lifestyle for cadres, one for the rest of society. But at the moment, at least, it is driven by the residual sentiments of self-sacrifice for Party elites while China marches towards its moment of national glory. After achieving that, the Xi leadership may well need to think of a new set of mobilising and incentivising inducements for its foot soldiers.

4

XI JINPING AND GLOBAL CHINA

The disciplined, renovated, newly motivated Communist Party under Xi Jinping, with its comprehensive approach and its mission to fulfil a great vision, is also a global party, albeit using a notion of globalisation increasingly with Chinese characteristics. Soon after coming to power, Xi convened a Politburo meeting in which he asked his colleagues to tell the China story better. Leaders felt that there was too little real understanding of China's intentions and that there were too many negative assumptions being made about the country by the outside world. Xi himself was aware that criticisms had been increasing during the Hu era, accusing the Party of having a silent leadership which was unwilling, or unable, to say what the world's second-largest economy wanted – or, more importantly, to rebut some of the wilder claims being made about its intentions. In the US, 'China Threat' narratives started to take hold. Chinese investment became problematic because it was suspected of masking overt political intentions. Confucius Institutes, set up in more than 500 foreign university campuses worldwide, became lightning rods for suspicion about China's intentions, with accusations made that they existed to promote benign, non-critical views of the country and were part of the work of the United Front, the department in the Party mandated to maintain linkages with overseas Chinese communities and other forces in society, and to promote the Party's vision as unified and acting in the interests of everyone.

Xi himself has become the chief diplomat in this effort to tell the China story. He has also sponsored an upgrade of international relations. In the Hu era, the foreign minister was usually one of the least prominent figures in the Party. (One prominent political figure in the UK even said to me, around 2011, 'When Henry Kissinger goes to Beijing, he now regards the head of their foreign ministry simply as the person who comes to open his car door as he goes in to see someone who actually matters!') Under Xi, Wang Yi currently holds the position and sits on the 350-strong Central Committee, but he is not even a member of the full Politburo, let alone the Standing Committee. State Councillor Yang Jiechi is the highest-ranked politician with oversight of international affairs – but did not sit on the full Politburo until 2017.

That has all changed now, with Yang being granted a place among the top 24. More relevantly, Wang Huning, who formerly worked as an academic in Shanghai and is a specialist in international relations with a background in the French language and the study of different notions of sovereignty, was one of the new promotions to the Standing Committee. Someone with no administrative experience to speak of (he has never been Party Secretary of a province, nor run a ministry), his greatest talent has been his ability to translate the ideas of Chinese political leaders over three generations from the time of Jiang into pithy slogans, and then to give these some theoretical basis and justification. Wang, a sallow, introverted figure who ceased to publish anything publicly once he disappeared behind the walls of the central leadership compound in 1994, reportedly constructed the idea of 'neo-authoritarianism'. He is the first international relations specialist to have been elevated, and his presence next to Xi shows that there is now a clear understanding of the importance of promoting a notion of global China.

In 2017, China has never been more interlinked with the outside world. Although Xi has been called the storyteller-in-chief within China, no Chinese leader has ever travelled as intensively or extensively outside the country's borders. It is remarkable that despite being imputed with vast powers domestically and involvement in every possible policy area, Xi also finds time to undertake this travel. And his trips abroad have not just been every now and again; in the five years since 2013, he has visited almost 50 countries and every continent on the planet. These have included such stalwart allies as

Russia and Indonesia, but also unexpected destinations like Fiji, Saudi Arabia and Chile. Xi has been to the UK and Germany, but also to the Czech Republic and New Zealand. He has visited the US several times, and Africa twice. The very fact that the Communist Party's most senior official has spent so much time flying to different global destinations testifies to one clear fact – that the outside world matters to China as never before, and has a massive stake and role in the country's future development. China continues to need its markets, its intellectual property, its competition (to make its own enterprises more effective) and its solidarity over issues that matter to it. But it is also now seeking something more than this – recognition from the outside world of its status.

The most explicit thing Xi Jinping Thought says about China's international vision is that it desires to be a great power. It was telling that during the 2017 Congress the Belt and Road Initiative (BRI) was written into the Party Constitution at the same time as Xi Thought. This vast idea, formally embracing more than 60 countries (but many more informally), is the first time in recent years that China has proactively spelt out an international vision. With China criticised in the first decade of the new century by the US and others for needing to be more explicit about its view of its own role in the world and its increasing power, the answer has come via the resurrection of the old idea of the Silk Roads, trading links that were first established in ancient times between the

Middle East, Europe and further afield into the various Chinese dynasties that existed over the centuries. There is plenty of argument about the historical form and intensity of such trading links, but the idea seemed to have had traction, with the great benefit of enabling China to present access to its market and stronger commercial relations as the easiest way to create an outward-looking narrative which avoids contentious areas like security or political alliances.

The BRI partially solves a conundrum for Xi's China. In the 1990s, under Jiang, there was a realisation that while the coastal parts of the country had managed to develop quickly via their logistical links with the outside world and more favourable locations for manufacturing, the central and western parts had fallen behind. Among other provinces, Tibet, Xinjiang, Gansu, Sichuan and Yunnan suffered from poor infrastructure, imperfect to non-existent public services, low levels of education and a raft of environmental, social and other issues. While Shanghai was enjoying more than US$ 10,000 per capita GDP by 2012, Gansu in the north-west had a mere US$ 3,000. There were also endemic issues such as educated people moving to more prosperous areas or even abroad, corruption and poor-quality governance, with the added complexity of local separatist movements in Xinjiang and Tibet, some of which developed into terrorism. In 2013 and 2014 Xi's administration had direct experience of this, with a car bomb set off in the hallowed space of Tiananmen Square, and vicious knife attacks by Islamist extremists on civilians in Kunming Station the following year.

Wang Jisi, an academic, first made the suggestion prior to 2012 that a simple solution to the development of the western regions would not need to involve large-scale investments from central government and domestic aid programmes, as had been proposed before, but could instead lie in exploiting the assets these regions have – their borders with countries like India, Russia and Pakistan, and the access this gave them to Central Asia and beyond. This would not only unlock potential new sources of growth, but also would diversify China's resource supply routes, which were largely dominated by a narrow band of sea in the Malacca Straits in the south that was easy for the US to control. With decent infrastructure and investment, China would be able to access oil and other resources across land, away from the interference of the US.

There were, of course, plenty of issues with this bold vision. It would involve opening up negotiations with countries that China had strained relations with (India, for instance, where there is still an unresolved border issue). China would also need to ensure that Russia, which regarded Central Asia as its backyard, did not become uneasy. And it would need to think hard about how best to deal with a region which it had had very little to do with in recent history. But under Xi the imperative, at least in this area, is to put plans into action and deal with the associated risks, rather than not to try at all because of potential problems.

The BRI also gives the Xi leadership a foreign policy narrative – one which involves the China Dream being exported. The mantra heard throughout the parts of the world affected by this grand vision is 'win–win', where everyone comes away with something. China goes to some lengths to say that its big idea is non-prescriptive, consensus-based and aimed at creating a multipolar world structure, one where the old dominance of a single power alone is consigned to history. While the actual projects related to the BRI have been few and far between at the time of writing, there has been plenty of interest and engagement. A vast conference in mid-2017 in Beijing was focused solely on the idea, with 27 heads of state or government in attendance. Vast sums of money have been mentioned, to be run through the New Silk Road Fund and the China Development Bank. Most importantly of all, the Asia Infrastructure Investment Bank (AIIB) was established in 2015, with more than 56 founding members.

A major project like the BRI showcases the strategic aspects of Xi's kind of rule and how its domestic tone impacts on its relationships abroad. At the same time as he was telling the Politburo meeting to 'tell the China story well' and to make sure the country was better heard and understood, he also stated in a speech to diplomats that China needed to take a more proactive stance in international affairs. As the world's second-largest economy, and one where so much was at stake, the country could no longer afford to remain passive and adhere to the famous Deng Xiaoping mantra of a couple of decades before, of 'keeping its head low and biding its time'. China had to start acting as itself – a major power with real influence.

Under Xi there has been a whole raft of anomalies to deal with in order to assume this new posture. Despite its strong focus on Chinese identity, Mao Zedong Thought did at least have a universalist component. Maoism was exported to developing countries in Africa and Latin America to help foment struggle against the capitalist world. In the early 1970s, China supported the revolutionary struggle in Vietnam between the Vietnamese Communists and the US, and in parts of the Third World, as it was called then. When Deng Xiaoping, newly released from house arrest, went to the United Nations in 1974 he declared that China had a leadership role over the Third World; after all, the term had first arisen in China. Maoist movements spread through parts of Asia, led by the inimitable thinking of the Chairman and disseminated mostly via the infamous 'Little Red Book', more properly called *Quotations from the Works of Mao Zedong*.

Xi Jinping Thought is not in the business of conversion like this. There are no illusions in Beijing that the outside world will suddenly embrace 'modernisation of socialism with Chinese characteristics for the new era'. The main reason for this is in the body of the slogan itself: how can the rest of the world adapt to ideas that are specifically tied to the country, and to notions of 'Chineseness' and its exceptional qualities? The approach from Xi's China is more about stressing the necessity of plurality, tolerance and granting his country legitimate status. That means demanding strategic space, particularly within China's periphery in the East and South China Seas and around its borders, in the contentious territory that it inhabits. The BRI and the AIIB, alongside older China-inspired or China-driven ideas like the Shanghai Cooperation Organisation or the Brazil, Russia, India, China and South Africa (BRICS) grouping, point in many different directions. But they are united in one fundamental characteristic. They are all entities which do not involve the US. For decades, the US has been present in China's world, almost hedging it in. Frustration at this was tangible during the Hu years when US troops were in South Korea, Japan and Afghanistan. The US created a rapprochement with Vietnam, and was deeply involved in the political changes in Myanmar. It seemed to have a finger in almost every pie. It became imperative to try and escape from the presence of the US almost everywhere China looked. This was done by spelling out clear China-centred core objectives, by placing greater stress on the need to maintain China's political system, which was now posited as part of its identity, and by making strong declarations of legitimate interest in islands in the South China Sea, and over the issue of Taiwan. Added to this was China's new ability to back up its demands with hard power – with a navy that, at least in terms of vessels, equals that of the US in power, even if it is many decades behind technologically.

Despite Xi Jinping Thought not being aimed at the outside world, Xi's China presents the world with three striking new aspects that Mao's China never did. The first is that throughout modern history China has been the underdog – and all too often the victim – either of colonial interference or of Japanese imperial aggression in World War II. In the Mao era it was regarded as introspective, closed off and 'the sick man of Asia'. But under Xi, the country is imputed with strength and purposefulness. This is a different set of qualities entirely and presents different challenges, both to China and to those that engage with it. China, for example, can no longer portray itself as the victim. Now it is often in the driving seat, particularly with the US under Donald Trump, who has created opportunities in terms of free-trade deals and environmental leadership that China never enjoyed before. The outside world, too, has plenty of experience of dealing with a weak China. But that entity no longer exists. China has the ability as never before to have an impact on the world around it. Adjusting to this new reality requires an immense change. With many countries stuck in the

'China Threat' mindset, it is unsurprising that they find the country's new position of power challenging. Some want to see no legitimate space for China unless granted to it by outsiders, while others fear that it will become the new 'global police' along the lines of the US, something it has shown little interest in being so far.

The second is that there is very little idea of what China might look like as a sea power. Since the brief (and very unusual) period almost six centuries ago, in which Ming China had been a seafaring nation under the eunuch admiral Zheng He, China had ceased to have a functional navy. It was only in the 1980s, when General Liu Huaqing led the creation of a modern naval force, that the country again had operational sea vessels. By 2017, it had managed to accrue more vessels than the US, although, as mentioned earlier in this chapter, technologically it remains far behind.

This ability to project power beyond its land borders gives China's influence a new dimension, which is already being felt in the South and East China Seas. In 2015, for the first time ever, China opened a military installation in Djibouti, on the east coast of Africa. Whether this massive amount of kit is ever likely to be used is another matter – it might be little more than symbolic. Paradoxically, since 1979 a strong China has also been one which has desisted from fighting with its neighbours, unlike when Mao was in charge. The real conflict now and in the future is being waged in the virtual world.

Here, China has had considerable success, infiltrating systems to such an extent that it was even accused of hacking into the German Chancellor's personal system and government systems in Australia. But China's navy and its visible declarations of power at least encourage the outside world to view the country in a new way. It is unlike the Chinas of the past. It has the ability, if necessary, to fight wars at sea.

The final new phenomenon is the most far-reaching and the most difficult to manage. No one, least of all China, quite understands or knows what a world run according to Chinese ideas should look like. In modern history, China has until recently been a marginalised, often forgotten power. Even in the new era of ambition and confidence under Xi, where domestically China has set its face resolutely against what it calls the proselytising Enlightenment values largely associated with the West, and where it resists what it labels as universalist discourses, particularly about national values, China has yet to present a model it wishes other countries to follow. Even in an era of doubts and confusion over the future of democracy, where China has been accused of trying to promote its own philosophy through entities like the Confucius Institutes, the country has been unable to propose a world order based on the values it seems to espouse – those of harmony, multipolarity, non-interference and balance – or indeed to adequately articulate them within its own borders, let alone in a way which can be understood outside China.

Can these values really be adopted as ideas according to which the world might run itself in the future? And is that what China ultimately wants?

One critique has been that in the first three decades of reform and opening up, China existed in two realms. On the one hand it benefited hugely from a rules-based, orderly and predictable international environment, one regulated by entities like the World Trade Organization (WTO) in a way which meant China could engage in international trade but also forge internal reforms through the use of external competition. At the same time, however, the country was able to stick to its mantra of exceptionalism, stating every step of the way that it was only undertaking these reforms and adopting these external rules according to the country's unique cultural circumstances. It was able to adopt this unique and sometimes subservient position while a relatively small economy, but as it grew economically and rose in diplomatic prominence, it became harder for the country to maintain the posture of a humble second-rank power simply following in the slipstream of others. In fact, China's own slipstream was more than enough to push everyone off course: because of its size and growth rate, through the very act of joining others' systems it changed these systems for everyone.

Under Xi Jinping, China is coming to terms with the idea of being a country with powers, a maker of rules as much as an observer of them. It is doing this in the face of a world around it which is at best ambiguous and at worst opposed to China's mission to have a greater and more defined space beyond its borders in which to exist. And under Trump, even more of this space has opened up. The problem now is that this moment of greater responsibility for Xi's China is also one of exposure. China never believed in the underlying principles on which the rules-based system it has engaged in internationally since 1978 is based. It does not subscribe to the same notion of law, as I discussed earlier in this book, nor the idea of freedoms such as those of expression or religion, nor to the free flow of information. The US-led post-World War II order which has prevailed until now is underpinned by these kinds of liberal values, and China has engaged with this system on the grounds of pragmatism and utility. It has gained a great deal from this engagement, and in some senses has fed off it. But now that the confidence in that system has been eroded, the question is whether China has a set of values it can replace the system with. More importantly, will the sceptical outside world accept them?

Xi Jinping Thought implicitly – and explicitly – recognises that tackling China's developmental challenges is situated in a global context, that its domestic and international issues are intimately linked. The 19th Party Congress, with its carefully managed choreography, was an event aimed at a domestic audience, but also at a world seeking some clues about the nature of Chinese power and how the country under Xi's leadership sees itself now. What the congress proved was that at this particular moment in time, approaching its achievement of the first centennial goal and the delivery of modernity with Chinese characteristics with the Communist Party in charge, China is a nation seeking validation and status. It wants recognition not just internally but also externally for its new-found position. It wants to be looked up to and admired. This is clear in its promotion of images of Xi and his leadership to the world around it, and in the way in which China tried during the congress to get external validation of its achievements. As Xi travels throughout the world, this act of validation continues. It is the theatre of affirmation, in which the hordes of applauding, smiling domestic audiences are replaced by foreigners basking in the glory of the rising China and its new greatness. This greatness with Chinese characteristics has to be recognised by outsiders to be meaningful. Perhaps this hunt and hunger for status, which the outside world already has, is the final thing that the country needs. It is of little value to achieve greatness without confirmation from others; the act needs two parties.

As in the realm of ideology, however, Xi's China is saddled with a stock of ideas and frameworks about the Party state's views of foreign policy that date back to the Maoist era. There are the Five Principles of Peaceful Coexistence, which date from the mid-1950s, a time when China was a small economy emerging from the devastation of war and largely diplomatically isolated. These principles stressed the kind of things a country in China's situation would want to preserve – non-interference by others, respect for its hard-won sovereignty, mutual recognition. By the 1980s, under the new leadership of Deng, with its stronger pragmatic strategic direction, the '24-character phrase' came in: keep a low profile, be willing to cooperate, and make time to deal with the country's significant internal challenges. In 2000, these were supplemented by Jiang Zemin's idea of a period of strategic opportunity that would last two decades. This was a somewhat edgier idea, one that hinted at a time in the future when China would be more able to dictate what it wanted. Towards the end of the Hu era, his chief diplomat Dai Bingguo suggested a set of core objectives – to preserve the country's current political system and the security of its territory, and to support stability while at the same time never relinquishing its just and right claims, in China's view, to territory in the South and East China Seas. This sat alongside the language about 'peaceful rise' sponsored at the time, which regularly appeared in leaders' speeches. China, it was made clear, would not be like other powers. It would not use its wealth to disrupt the international system. It would rise on the back of consensus and harmony. That was the theory, at least.

At the heart of these various iterations – and the core issue that Xi and his colleagues have to wrestle with – is the simple fact that their country is now immensely prominent, wealthy and influential. It has assets and investments abroad, and supply chains that reach across the globe. Unlike in Mao's time, it has capital and logistical bonds with the world around it, and exists in a profoundly international environment. It was for this reason that Xi spoke for the first time ever at the World Economic Forum, held in Davos in early 2017, in defence of the system of globalisation seen as under threat from the new Trump presidency. The world's last major communist one-party state was now the most powerful defender of a process until then associated with multiparty democracies. The irony was a rich and arresting one.

This new position has given China an almost schizophrenic diplomatic identity. Its foreign policy formulations over the last seven decades have wavered between portraying itself as a small, marginal player and representing itself as one which regards itself as the centre of a new world order after its rise to 'peaceful power' status. Under Xi, China has validated its act of dreaming about its glorious future role, even though this sometimes comes across as hubris. But there is a practical issue arising from the accrual of former diplomatic positions which are now located in a wholly new environment. China is a country which has the sixth-largest amount of investment abroad. It is the world's second-largest importer, and its largest trading partner, doing business with more than 120 countries. Turmoil and unrest in its key partner countries now cause it problems. In the Middle East, from where it gets half its imported oil, domestic issues have a major effect on the security of its supplies. How tenable, therefore, is a position of non-interference when China has to take a stance and intervene, even if only to protect its own interests? The stance of a bystander is fine when it comes to issues that do not matter much, but when they are of immense importance to its citizens it cannot just stand aside. In 2011, for example, 37,000 Chinese nationals had to be repatriated from Libya when civil war broke out. And in 2017, China was accused of being the final arbiter behind the fall of Mugabe in Zimbabwe. The country was also pressured to be a dealmaker in Myanmar over unrest there by the EU, China and others.

Xi's era is the era of global China. That in itself would indicate the need for a new diplomatic language. China can no longer pretend that it is a mouse when everyone else knows it is an elephant. The disjuncture between its own language – about its limited capacities and diplomatic potency – and that of the world outside its borders which sees nothing but expressions of power, pushiness and force, is a severe and unsettling one. China always seems to be aiming for win–win outcomes, doing asymmetrical deals where it is the perpetual victor and placing its own interests before a more altruistic, generous posture towards the wider world. It has the mindset of a minor power that sees itself as vulnerable but the physical capacity of a superpower.

With the Belt and Road Initiative, and in the way Xi speaks, he is at least starting to face this disjunction to find the voice of a China that is authentically global and can speak to the world as such. But there is a further question, to which no one will know the answer for some time. China now has the opportunity and space to be a global player, and many countries in the world are even ready to embrace it in doing this. However, can China, with its exceptionalism and its belief in its own exclusive set of values, act as a power that recruits, engages and involves others, as the US did in its heyday? Or is the country fated to be forever the great outsider, creating a system that is self-serving and where everything is about utility and pragmatism, and which never leads to shared ideals and more global identities? That model would be an old-fashioned one, a return in many ways to the priority of the nation state and an attempt to recruit the wider world to a mission centred on China and only China. It might work for a while, but not for long. There would be huge issues around sustainability. This approach would place Chinese sovereignty and agency in a privileged position, recreating the hierarchy of the past that China claims it wants to move away from. A communist Confucian global order has always seemed fanciful, despite Xi's eloquence. It may well prove a complete chimera more quickly than anyone expected.

5

XI AND POLITICAL REFORM

Every time a new Chinese leader appears, there is excited babble about his being a 'hidden reformer', meaning that he will emulate Mikhail Gorbachev and produce a raft of ideas which will turn China into a multiparty entity more like European or North American countries, allowing it to finally breathe in the elixir of freedom and join the global community of the free, proving that history did end in the 1990s and that the anomaly of the one-party system's survival in China has finally been resolved.

This desire to see a China politically like the West (where 'the West' is a metaphor for the 88 multiparty democracies in which groups need to compete for power, as defined by Freedom House, a US-based non-governmental organisation that monitors these things) has been around for a long time. Deng himself was regarded as a potential liberaliser – despite him not once indicating any wavering in his support for the Leninist one-party principle and the privileges of the Communist Party which he had been a member of since he was 16, and which he had sacrificed so much for. Although Deng was placed on the cover of *Time* magazine not once but twice in the 1980s as a potential bringer of both economic and political reforms in China, this fanciful idea was to be rudely dispelled when he reacted so fiercely and decisively to the 1989 uprising.

A similar desire to see all of Deng's successors as potential reformers has remained. Jiang Zemin, Hu Jintao and then Xi himself were watched closely to see if they were potential Gorbachevs. This ignored all the evidence that showed that the USSR's reforms were regarded with horror in China and their outcomes (collapse of the Party and creation of a chaotic multiparty successor) viewed as largely negative. The chances of Xi Jinping being a reformer of this model therefore were low to non-existent. And nothing that he did before coming to power would have led attentive observers to think otherwise.

There are deep and complex reasons for this. China's complicated nature, its highly fragmented economy and its history of being afflicted by turbulence and disunity mean that its political leaders are extremely distrustful of risk. Like Machiavelli, they stand by the mantra that to trust is good, but to control is better. Those who are chosen by the Party to lead provinces, as Xi did for over a decade, are largely valued as risk and crisis managers. They live, breathe and work in an environment saturated with memories of former crises and collapses which stretch back hundreds of years. Environmentally, China is prone to earthquakes (the one in Tangshan near Beijing in 1976 killed a quarter of a million people), floods (from the Yellow and Yangtze Rivers) and other natural disasters. But it also remembers the human catastrophes, from the Taiping rebellion of 1850 to 1864 that ended in the deaths of 20 to 30 million Chinese, to the savage final years of the Civil War of 1946–9 and the reappearance of deep social divisions during the Cultural Revolution. Knowledge of this history is a given for elite leaders, and they are therefore highly sensitive to any notion of instability and the threat this brings. Their main skill is in managing situations to ensure that chaos does not return.

This does not mean, however, that they never contemplate change, but they do need sound reason to do so. The 1978 reforms were bold, but prompted and justified by the deep crisis that Mao's failed economic policies had brought about. There was never any intention to extend them to the political realm without a similarly compelling rationale. Any political changes have only been made when, in the minds of the elite leaders, there is a sound economic reason to do so. That has never included multiparty democracy because of the potential uncertainty that such a change brings with it.

Xi is from a generation exposed to constant pressure from the outside world, particularly the US, to consider adopting political reforms. To leaders like him, the whole engagement process has an underlying motive which is not in China's best interests – a desire to force the country, through closer economic integration with the outside world, to also use some of its models of governance. Money from NGOs, particularly those in the US, like the National Democratic Institute, went to supporting grass-roots entities in China. The Ford Foundation and Carter Center became active. The EU supported village election projects. For a few years in the late 1990s and early years of the new millennium there seemed moments of liberalism. But even under the low-key and diffident Hu Jintao, there were persistent clampdowns. This only intensified when the Arab Spring began around 2010. China observed the Western mission creep in Libya, where Gaddafi was unceremoniously toppled from power and other nations in the region fell into the sort of chaos it so feared. This was compounded by the Colour Revolutions in independent satellite states of the former Soviet Union and the eruption of protests in 2014 in a democratic Taiwan. Finally, democracies were embarrassed by their poor governance, which led to financial meltdown for many after the great financial crisis of 2008. It didn't seem that capitalist countries could even take good care of their own capital under their sloppy systems. At the elite level, Chinese scepticism about the merits of adopting Western models of governance started to seep down deeper into the Party.

Since Xi Jinping has come to power, the wholesale disappearance of any real notion of political reform has been striking. In his speech at the opening of the 19th Party Congress, while he mentioned 'modernisation', 'mission' and other keywords multiple times and covered a huge number of different areas and issues, democracy barely got a mention. This is particularly striking because his predecessor Hu Jintao used the word more than 60 times when he spoke at the opening of the 2007 Congress. The new ideological formulation of 'modernisation of socialism with Chinese characteristics', which is such a major part of Xi Jinping Thought, involves reform – and yet reform in the most important area of all, the political, has been dealt with largely by silence. The proposition that China could create under the Party a dynamic new kind of mixed, higher-value economy, using a model of governance which has largely remained unchanged in the last seven decades, needs attention. Would this even be possible? And if so, what would it mean for our general Western theories of modernisation, where economic change is usually linked so closely to political change, and where the two are regarded as being inseparable?

A distinctive feature of the Xi era has been the muscular approach to any discourse implying that China might be embracing Western forms of governance. An internal Party document called Document Number Nine (such official Party edicts are numbered sequentially, beginning from the first document issued in the January of each year), leaked in 2014 by a journalist (who was harshly treated when her 'crime' was discovered), stipulated that academics should not promote ideas like support for Western-style divisions of power, constitutionalism, federalism or bicameral parliamentary systems like that used in Westminster in the UK. This aversion to the constellation of ideas bundled under the label 'Western liberalism' was nothing new, however. Since the 1980s, Deng Xiaoping had warned of the problem: when you open windows to let fresh air in, flies come in too! Spiritual pollution and bourgeois liberalisation campaigns were sporadically organised against figures like Fang Lizhe, the prominent astrophysicist, who went from being a Party member to being a trenchant critic of the Party. He was exiled in 1989. In the 1990s, the pressure continued, with a major clampdown against the China Democracy Party in 1998 when it tried to file for formal recognition, and against the Falun Gong religious group a year later. Even in the years of rampant, almost giddy growth under Hu Jintao, the Party produced stinging criticisms of Western political models, most neatly encapsulated in the 'Six Whys' document issued in 2009 – why China would never adopt a multiparty model, for instance, and why it would never allow courts to challenge the legitimacy of the Party. Document Number Nine was therefore another iteration of this.

What has been distinctive about the Xi era regarding discussion of political reform has been the almost complete lack of any real debate. In the past, there was some space – albeit highly restricted – to consider the viability of liberalising politics in China. Yu Keping, a scholar official in the Central Committee Translation and

Compilation Bureau, produced a book in 2010 called *Democracy Is a Good Thing*. Village elections were mandated in a national law in 1998, allowing 3 million such multi-candidate events to take place, and in the early years of the millennium the Hu administration came up with the concept of 'intra-Party democracy', where the Communist Party carried out in-house debates on reform, trying to make itself more accountable and transparent. Both of these initiatives have largely ceased under Xi. Village elections are held, but hardly have any real meaning. The attempt to have them gravitate to township status and higher levels of governance has ended. The Party is now about unity and discipline. Intra-Party democracy comes across as an alien idea, with only one brief, almost passing mention in Xi's 2017 speech to the 19th Congress.

Xi Jinping Thought is a political ideology. And the Xi leadership is firmly focused, as already suggested, on ensuring the Party is a political entity, has a clear political programme and is involved solely in the work of politics. Unlike with economic reform, though, there have so far been no moves to spell out how political change might be effected. China is a country of almost daily physical, social and cultural change, and yet we are asked to believe that in the domain of politics – one of the most complex, sensitive and changeable areas of human behaviour – things are static. The Party will perpetually exist as it does now: unchallenged and unchanging. This seems remarkable, and unlikely.

Before being tempted to accept this proposition, there are a number of different issues to consider. Firstly, no one really knows what the Xi leadership's attitude towards political reform might be – or, at least, what his personal attitude is. We can become easily distracted by the excitement of imagining that the Party will embrace organised political opposition. There is not a shred of evidence, however, that this is likely to happen any time soon. But there are other options – along the lines, for instance, of what happened in Taiwan in the 1980s, where there was a relaxation of the rules, rather than the formal acceptance of more pluralism in politics, a decade or so before institutional change took place. Maybe a one-party system with competition within itself might be possible; indeed, it is likely that this is the preferred option of the highly cautious current leaders of the People's Republic. All we know is that under Xi, it is not an issue of them having said no to political reform. They have said nothing about it at all. That betrays a more doubtful, hesitant posture – not an adamantly opposed one.

Secondly, there is the issue of timing. As this book has already made clear, the Xi era is shaping up to be one with a sense of historic portentousness. The achievement of the first centennial goal in 2021 will also mark the moment when China starts to deliver its hitherto unfulfilled promise of rejuvenation. Risking this moment for reforms which are complex, where the outcomes are uncertain and where current demands for them are not absolutely crucial, would be foolhardy. China's once-in-a-hundred-years opportunity could be thwarted, and the Xi leadership would immediately go down in history as a failure. It is not surprising, therefore, that there is so little discussion of political reform. It is simply too complex to address fully at present. China continues to wait for the day when reform might be opportune. That might come incrementally, or as a result of crisis. But it does not mean there is not a strong notion that this area will need attention at some point.

And thirdly, there is the real possibility that there is no consensus on this issue within the Party. There is, after all, an uneasy truce between more leftist and liberal forces on the relatively more straightforward problem of the role of the market in the economy, as discussed earlier in this book. When it comes to options for political reform, there are likely to be even deeper fractures. This reinforces the arguments that on this matter we should not assume silence is a sign of strength and unity. It might equally be an indication of vulnerability and hidden divisions.

In this largely silent atmosphere, civil society activists and human rights lawyers, among others, have been given brutal treatment. While the Jiang and Hu eras were hardly golden ages of tolerance and liberalism, under Xi the restrictions have grown even tighter, and punishments have increased for those who are deemed to have violated the unwritten (or sometimes written and harsh) rules. Liu Xiaobo, the 2010 Nobel Peace Prize winner, died of cancer eight years into his 13-year sentence for state subversion, despite international pressure for him to be treated abroad. His wife, Liu Xia, who has never been found guilty of any crime in any Chinese court, remains largely incommunicado, despite fears about her mental and physical health.

The Xi leadership believes in rule by law. That at least is clear from the commitment that it made in the 2014 Party Plenum, the fifth, where a whole communiqué was devoted to the subject of legal reform. For the core constituency that Xi needs to keep onside, the emerging middle class, some predictability and reassurance about their property and land rights is important. For these people, their largest investment, as is the case with inhabitants of capitalist economies, is in their apartments and (for those lucky enough to have the money to buy them) houses. Loans and mortgages are available, but usually must be paid back over a maximum of 15 years. Property in Shanghai in 2016 was more expensive than in a city as infamously pricey as Sydney. As *The Economist* made clear in an article on 13 October the same year ('When a bubble is not a bubble'), the Chinese housing market was perhaps the world's largest – and most overpriced – single resource. For the commuting, service-sector-working, hard-pressed emerging Chinese bourgeoisie, legal reassurances over the security of their most important assets matter as much to them as in any other jurisdiction. The same goes for the development of commercial law, where (as discussed earlier) despite the establishment of a functioning legal system its implementation had previously been poor, and all too often politics overrode clearly written rules.

For Xi's China, law has its place – and its place is placating the new members of the bourgeoisie. But this does not back up the idea of supporting activist legal workers who are trying to promote political rather than legal agendas. There, the tolerance is low to non-existent. During the Colour Revolutions that toppled regimes in the former Soviet Union satellite states after 2000, Chinese leaders concluded that one of the principal causes of unrest had been lawyers with political agendas challenging the legitimacy of the political parties in power. Alongside this group of lawyers were civil society activists, who were also accused of having ulterior motives. Xi's focus on the primacy of the Party means there can be no distraction or dilution of its legitimacy. In the Hu era, figures like Xu Zhiyong and Gao Zhisheng were allowed some space, the former initially setting up a think tank called Open Constitution to discuss some elements of constitutional reform and open governance and the latter representing contentious cases like Falun Gong practitioners. Both were to fare badly. Gao was taken in for the first time in 2007, disappeared, then released briefly under Xi before being removed from public life once more. There were well-documented claims that he had been badly abused and tortured while in detention.

Xu, whose activities were regarded until the era of Xi as largely non-contentious, was one of more than 200 lawyers and law-related professionals who were taken in during 2015 and 2016 and questioned, put under house arrest and otherwise intimidated. He was rewarded with a four-year prison sentence, backdated to 2014, for public disorder offences, finally being released in 2017.

Xi's China is an anomaly. In some ways, there is a defensible rationale behind its desire to increase clarity on legal restrictions and regulations, and to update the statute books. The foreign non-governmental organisations law introduced in 2016, which requires all such NGOs to register with the Ministry of Public Security or the police before conducting any activities in mainland China, is a case in point – a codification, some argue, of practices that already existed and therefore needed to be part of a more transparent framework. Many of these practices may have struck some as undesirable and restrictive – the demand, for instance, that all international NGOs based in China have two official bodies sponsoring them, rather than only one – but at least they were putting down in black and white what many, in fact, had already been expected to do. This has created a kind of clarity, albeit one which is unpleasant. But Xi's demands for Party officials to remain loyal and disciplined are now also becoming imperatives aimed at lawyers and human rights defenders. For the world outside, too, Xi has created a sense of ambiguity. His is an administration which has taken seriously the implementation of many of its environmental laws, largely unheeded until he came to power, punishing companies and governments that fail to meet standards required in law. For the global fight against man-made climate change, this is surely a good thing. At the same time, as mentioned earlier in this chapter, environmentalist groups, civil society actors who agitate for more accountability and journalists whose stories fall foul of the increasingly assertive censors risk real reprisals – often extremely harsh ones. For dissidents and human rights lawyers, China under Xi has become a tough place to live. Even worse, the public atmosphere fuelled by nationalism and the hunt for 'great nation' status means that activists in more marginal areas are even further ostracised by the toxic claim that they are 'enemies within'. They are painted as trying to sabotage the country's great moment of rebirth and return it to the history of humiliation and pain it is so keen to emerge from, and which it now has such a good chance to put to rest.

Foreign governments seeking to enter dialogue with China on human rights issues now face an even more confident – and categorically dismissive – opponent. World leaders have remained silent on human rights issues; for example, during his visit to Beijing in November 2017, US president Donald Trump avoided discussion of the subject, despite standard practice being for the leader of the world's most powerful democracy to place pressure on China to address what are perceived to be its major human rights problems. In this respect, Trump's transactional presidential style suits Xi's China, which no longer wishes to be lectured on governance or values. Where boundaries become more blurred, and the situation gets more complex, is when non-Chinese nationals end up in jail in China and experience its harsh criminal justice system. Unlike commercial law, criminal law is circumscribed by a number of difficult issues, such as presumption of guilt until proven innocent and the proclivity of agents of the state to use violence to extract confessions or enforce obedience, despite many attempts to rein in the latter. Peter Humphrey, a British corporate investigator and long-term resident of China, was to get first-hand experience of this when he was detained as a result of a case against a client he was working for, medical multinational GSK. Humphrey was paraded on television in a prison suit and then placed in jail after a brief trial, languishing there until lobbying and his own medical condition secured his release. For lower-profile Chinese nationals, treatment is likely to be far worse.

Much of Xi's campaign has been based on strengthening institutions and procedures, and creating a sense of predictability. But he himself stands accused of undermining these. Xi's mode of governance privileges the use of informal groupings of people in order to make decisions. These gatherings, known as Small Leading Groups, have been in existence since the 1950s, and are made up of selected leaders from the Party who come together to make key policy decisions that the government then has to implement. The groups cut across the Party and the administration unlike any others, but they are also largely opaque, and their deliberations are mostly unknown. Of the dozen or so such groups that have been identified – for instance, foreign affairs, comprehensive deepening of reform or the newly created national security committee – Xi chairs over half. He has been called the 'Chairman of Everything'. Around him there is a group of close, trusted advisers who are not members of a faction as such but people Xi has worked with and who evidently have gained his trust and understand him. Ding Xuexiang, who was Xi's personal secretary when he was in Shanghai and who was elevated to the Politburo in 2017, is one example. Another is Li Zhanshu, who was raised even higher, into the Standing Committee. Liu He, a man Xi called in front of one visiting dignitary his most important economic adviser, also sits on the full Politburo. These people are largely devoid of provincial leadership experience. But they are skilled bureaucratic administrators, and they are likely to obediently implement Xi's political instructions.

The Chairman of Everything is in charge of a party that has put a lot of effort into trying to institutionalise its own systems, at least since the era of Mao. The painful experience of its vulnerability to an all-powerful leader at that time led to the introduction of a raft of reforms, including more regular congresses, age limits and attempts to sort out rules of succession. As has already been shown, the last of these has proved the most difficult. For the Xi leadership, then, there is a clear quandary. On the one hand, investing so much in a charismatic, all-encompassing leader is regarded as creating reassurance and clarity. It might not be the case that they have the scope of powers they seem to; after all, how can one man decide everything in a country as vast as China is today? But enough people believe that Xi is in charge, and that gives things a sense of order and unity. The downside to this approach is the proclivity of the Chinese system to gift so much formal and informal power to individuals that they start to overshadow everyone else. They become like trees in a forest clearing, under which nothing is able to grow because of the lack of light. And Xi's powers now seem to have their own dynamic. How will the Party, an institution that needs to survive and prosper after Xi has moved on, be able to sustain the narrative of being a well-governed, autonomous entity when it appears to have been pushed back into an era where succession rules – albeit unwritten ones – might either be unheeded or suspended entirely?

The Xi era, and Xi Jinping Thought, seem consistent in areas like foreign relations, economy, and administrative and political reform in one particular characteristic – their hybridity. Today's market exists alongside state restrictions, but an assertive, strong China has also taken on more international responsibilities, and a Party embracing some forms of rule of law also tries to make categorically clear that these don't apply directly to the Party and its operations. In some areas, therefore, the Xi leadership is about creating a new social contract with an emerging middle class – one where they get a better deal in terms of certain rights and economic freedoms, and where their aspiration to live in a rich, powerful country is finally being satisfied. But all of this is happening alongside a lack of meaningful public discussion of political reform itself, and where there is increasing evidence that Xi is aiming for a presidency and leadership that will last beyond the year 2022, the year he once was expected to retire. At that point, will the argument – that his great mission has only been partly achieved and that he needs more time to achieve it – carry weight? And, in a system so devoid of long-established protocols and limits to authority, will he really be able to avoid becoming power-crazed and starting to act increasingly like a neo-Mao autocrat?

There is one final point I would like to make in this chapter about the nature of politics and the kind of leadership Xi sits at the heart of in China today. Much of his work has been about clearing away those with vested interests, reinforcing loyalty to the Party and getting rid of any hints of tribalism and factionalism which might erode the Party's collective identity. Personal networks, where links between family members and associates trumped everything else, had been a curse to Chinese organisations for a long time, and Xi's new leadership line-up in 2017 is one from which no easy factional message can be drawn. There are people allegedly linked to the Shanghai group (Han Zheng, a city native and its former mayor and Party secretary), the China Youth League group (around Li Keqiang) and the princelings (Xi himself). But the overriding impression is that in this leadership there are no easy boxes into which to fit people. They are mostly individuals who have held high-level bureaucratic, administrative or performance responsibilities and who have a proven track record of performing well under pressure. Wang Yang, for instance, highly regarded as an economist, had been Party secretary of the southern province of Chongqing and then of the municipality of Guangdong, two massive local government areas. Zhao Leji had been head of the all-powerful Organisation Department before elevation. Some had a record of working with Xi (Li Zhanshu and Wang Huning, for instance). Even at the level of policy commonalities there are no obvious links. Wang Yang is regarded as a liberal, as is Han Zheng. But Li Zhanshu and Zhao Leji are more difficult to pigeonhole.

Is Xi – the leader who is anti-networks, against narrowly focused linkages, whose core message is, above all, to try and restore the Party's collective identity and the supremacy of commitments and allegiances to it – actually creating a system of patronage based solely on links back to himself? It would be an extraordinary piece of daylight manipulation if he is legislating so fiercely against this behaviour elsewhere in the body politic, making clear this sort of activity is not part of the modernisation project China needs as it tries to observe objective, predictable rules, and yet undertaking it himself. Perhaps he has some privileged strategic reasons for doing this, such as the pragmatic need to create discipline and to inevitably focus everything on one individual. Even so, this strategy carries obvious risks. Power is a mighty drug; Mao Zedong proved that. Xi's China is on many levels a paradox, and that paradox is present right at the heart of Xi's style of leadership – the modernising leader, promoting a Party which is above networks and connections around individuals, who himself is served by colleagues working at the highest level who are only linked by the fact that they have worked closely with him.

6

XI JINPING THOUGHT

At the start of this book, I referred to Xi Jinping standing in the Great Hall of the People on 18 October 2017. This was expected to be the moment he would consolidate his power and reveal his true intentions for China. But history was not so easy to shake off. Standing with him on the podium were his predecessors. To one side of Xi was the immaculately still and inscrutable Hu Jintao, whose personnel Xi has been largely removing from the administration and whose legacy Xi has been deftly dismantling. If Hu was perturbed he did not show it, maintaining the same impenetrable exterior that he had sustained over a decade in power. On his other side, however, was a more distracting sight: Jiang Zemin, nearly 90 years of age, attending despite several confident reports of his demise over the previous years. Jiang stole the show by either yawning visibly at several points, or occasionally lifting up a large white light-up magnifying glass, which he used to stare, apparently bewildered, at the paper copy of Xi's speech. His networks too, along with those of his own children and close family, had been touched by the anti-corruption struggle.

Despite these distractions, Xi certainly acted and sounded like a man in complete control. But the two figures either side of him were a reminder of something other than just the past leaderships and the shadows they cast. Jiang, for all the brickbats he had received, had managed to stabilise China after the existential crisis of 1989 and the student uprising at the time. Together with Zhu Rongji, he had undertaken a series of state-owned-enterprise reforms which had fundamentally restructured the Chinese economy. He had secured the 2008 Olympics for the country, and managed to get it accepted into the World Trade Organization. He had removed military interference from the business sphere, and passed a new set of village election reforms. These were significant achievements, despite his reputation as an avuncular lightweight. Hu's achievements, on the other hand, were more straightforward. He had taken command of a country and in a decade quadrupled the size of its economy and overseen its successful entry into the WTO. He had held a successful Olympics in Beijing and effectively handled the fallout from the Tibetan and Xinjiang uprisings in 2008 and 2009 respectively. He had also been part of the leadership that had seen off the worst impacts of the global financial crisis in 2008, mitigating their effects in China.

Jiang and Hu had bequeathed to Xi a China with a huge economy, with several reforms already successfully implemented. Xi was able to speak with such a sense of mission that day because of the achievements of his predecessors. On the question of his own accomplishments, it was a little less easy to be complacent. Of the three men, Xi had seen the weakest growth and the slowest programme of reforms. To critics, his achievements were still in the pipeline – he was a leader still untested by any major crisis. In that sense, he still had to bid for his place in history.

It is for that reason that he was generous in his acknowledgement of all the historic achievements of his predecessors, and spoke of his leadership as part of a continuum going back not only to 1978 but to the period before this, when the Communist Party first took the mantle of modernity in China and developed the concept of socialism with Chinese characteristics. The Party mission was to ensure that this set of ideas was honoured and developed, not jettisoned and abandoned. In his report at the congress, socialism with Chinese characteristics resembled for Xi the core of a religious belief, a faith that had to be conveyed to and shared with all Chinese people, and of which he was the high priest. He simply referred to it as a 'great cause'. It was the cause upon which – with the Party in control – the story of China's final rejuvenation hung.

So what can we take away from this epic speech on 18 October? What are the core attributes of Xi Jinping

Thought and of the modernisation of socialism with Chinese characteristics? Where does this belief system stand now as Xi heads with the Party towards achievement of its first centennial goal, the delivery of a middle-income country by 2021? How long can the system hold up?

Firstly, both the Party in general and Xi Jinping Thought go to great lengths to stress that they are people-centred. That links them with the Hu Jintao era, when leaders talked about 'taking people as the base', making sure their aspirations were met and that the Party was relevant to their lives and to the concrete mission of delivering a better life for them. A theme throughout this book has been how the Party has often veered towards becoming a lobby group for itself, a club of vested interests whose chief priority has been to serve itself and to ensure its own survival. There is scepticism about what the Party means when it declares that it 'serves the people', and what this term 'the people' might actually mean. Xi referred in his speech to the old idea of the United Front, where all groups across society at least acknowledged the Party's unifying function. There are also other sections where he talked of all people being consulted. The Party under Xi has become the servant, above all, of the growing middle class, with its aspirations and its hunger for a good life. But he also talked of those left behind, those still living in absolute poverty.

People-centred policies attempt to give the Party a human face and break free of the idea that there is a chasm between itself and those it serves. Is it possible, however, for someone surrounded by the appurtenances of power, as Xi was that day, to reach beyond their confines into all parts of society around them? Before Xi came to power, there were rumours of him once appearing at the side of a street in Beijing, being picked up by a taxi driver and taken to the gates of the government compound, Zhongnanhai. On another, more documented occasion he appeared in a humble snack bar in Beijing having a simple meal. The propagandists like these images of very powerful people appearing to be just like everyone else. But anyone with even peripheral experience of officialdom in China knows how remote and out of reach those in power are. The fundamental problem, of lots of power concentrated in the hands of only a few, remains. Just four officials at the Ministry of Finance in Beijing decide how central funds are to be disbursed to the provinces. Figures like Xi live in a world where they never take a plane with ordinary people, or travel by car along roads that have not first been swept of other travellers by a security detail. There is the spectacle of serving the people, and of humility, but how real is it? And does the word 'people' figure as anything more than an abstraction in Xi's discourse?

Perhaps the most realistic conclusion we can draw is that unlike in the era of Mao, the people, the emerging middle class, now have greater agency. They are the producers of wealth and innovation. In a subtle way, the power dynamics have changed. It is the desires of the people which guide the Party and affect the way it formulates policy. And in the end, it is the people's dissatisfactions and discontent which will pose the greatest risk of the Party being swept from power. 'Taking people as the base' is an indirect way of admitting that fundamental political reality.

From this one focal point, much of the other elements of Xi Jinping Thought flow. The Party has to deliver 'socialist law with Chinese characteristics'; it has to respond to people's aspirations, improve governance and articulate a strong unifying vision which it believes in (or at least gives the appearance of believing in). The Party is where the articulation of domestic goals links with the outside world. It controls and disciplines the military, ensuring they are servants of the national mission rather than having a vested interest in their own power and threatening politicians with their control of force. Through the anti-corruption struggle, Xi has purged the General Affairs Office, the top command entity of the People's Liberation Army (PLA), of many of its former personnel and put in place a new group of military leaders. The symbolism of that alone has made clear where in the Party the real orders come from – the civilian arm, not the military one. For the PLA, their function is simple, as Xi has said: to fight wars. But those wars can only be part of a national mission, not an aside to demonstrate the military's own potency. And in many ways, the construction of China's vast navy is a symbolic act. China has had no combat experience since 1979. It has been most successful in the hidden space of the cyber world rather than in demanding operations of hard power. There a war is already going on, and China has been winning. Why fight physical wars when you can conquer through data, trade and covert infiltration? Xi declared that day that China was a global power, and implied that it should not be ashamed of this fact: it had earned the legitimate right to this status. But in addition to this, he also stated that the Party, on behalf of the Chinese nation, could articulate a sense of common destiny – a vision for humanity and for itself, the notion of a global China which the world could embrace, and ultimately become part of.

All of this is dependent on one strategic necessity – strong, unified leadership under the Communist Party. For a nation afflicted by nightmares of disunity and fragmentation, where mentioning the word 'instability' is a great taboo, declaring so strongly that the Party is solving this problem through its own hard-won and well-preserved unity was key. Several times in his 18 October speech Xi stressed unity: unified leadership from the Politburo down to the Central Committee, to the Party and Party membership, and then out to society. The Party would obey laws, strengthen its institutions, build self-discipline and observe ideological purity. More importantly, it would be a unifying cultural and ethical entity, the place where social and civic values would mix, where modernity channelled through Marxism–Leninism and Mao Zedong Thought would meet the great tradition of what Xi calls 'five thousand years of culture and history'.

The hybridity of Xi Jinping Thought has already been mentioned in the previous chapter. But the Party now is about much more than economic processes and building the primary stage of socialism. It must articulate a set of values and a culture which conveys the country's confidence and standing. It needs to create a set of civic values in a society reeling from fast-paced change over the last three decades. The core socialist values Xi refers to and which were discussed earlier in this book mix notions of harmony, tolerance and responsibility together with those of justice, legality and order. At the end of the Qing dynasty, Kang Youwei, one of the great visionary reformers who had attempted to map out a path of peaceful modernisation for China, had written of the 'great unity' that needed to be forged from all the diversity in China. But despite this, the Communist Party has often been divisive. In 1949, it had set out a series of values that were often antagonistic towards those of traditional Chinese society. Xi himself refers to the idiom of the 'three great mountains' – feudalism, imperialism and colonisation. Under Mao, the old world was to be upended and destroyed. 'Smash the Four Olds' became one of the most powerful movements during the Cultural Revolution, with many monuments to past leaders desecrated, including Confucius's tomb in Qufu, Shandong province. But in post-Mao China, the introduction of pragmatism, the collapse of people's faith in the ideology of Marxism–Leninism and the failure to impose the Party – through means of communes and other collectivist projects – as a great family in place of the natural, extended one marked a moment of ethical readjustment and reconciliation. Xi's Party is that of a great nation, and that nation has its ancient culture, which must be respected and taken advantage of. The marrying of Party values and outlooks with that of China's own history has been spectacularly achieved simply by use of the statement 'with Chinese characteristics'. Xi even speaks of 'think tanks with Chinese characteristics', as though there is a specifically Chinese way of thinking.

Xi Jinping Thought is comprehensive, he declared; it is incremental, a development of what has gone before. It is a hybrid, a means of achieving unity between tradition and modernity, taking elements from Marxism and Chinese traditions and aiming at practical outcomes. Most importantly, it is idealistic, something that is there to deliver a vision – a society that by 2035 (the year which according to Xi in his speech on 18 October 2017 will mark the fulfilment of the first state of socialist modernisation in China) will be well on its way to 2049, and the second centennial goal.

Like its predecessors Mao Zedong Thought and Deng Xiaoping Theory, Xi Jinping Thought is meant to be the perfect distillation of theoretical perspicacity and practical experience. But it is also geared towards outcomes that are ideal and, at times, almost utopian. Society is a massive machine, where the right inputs and prompts will produce the best outcomes. People are the same – a combination of forces and ingredients that need alignment to create new model citizens. The government's role under the Party is to do the balancing and measuring, to make sure things are assembled correctly and the machine works. As philosophers Gilles Deleuze and Félix Guattari put it, the human unconscious is a 'desiring-machine'. The aggregation of humans, therefore, makes society a vast desiring factory. The challenges on the way to creating a perfect society, as Xi outlined them in 2017, were well understood, and frequently repeated in leaders' speeches: unbalanced and inadequate development; a deficit in innovation; a vulnerable natural environment, which to a large extent has been destroyed or depleted; poverty; and lack of civic-mindedness. To these problems could be added formidable ones around demographics (China's ageing population) and health (the rise of chronic diseases). In addition, the country also faces the sorts of mental health and well-being issues that have been affecting the developed world for decades.

For Xi Jinping Thought, as for its predecessor thought systems, China was still at the preliminary stage of socialism. It still needed to stick to what was called in a slogan from the era of Mao and then Deng about Party core values 'The Four Cardinal Principles': adherence to socialism; the democratic dictatorship of the masses; the leadership of the Party; and observing Marxism–Leninism and Mao Zedong Thought. The modernisation of socialism with Chinese characteristics for the new era, the thought system written into the Party constitution, envisaged a society which by 2035 would offer Chinese people the delivery, in most respects, of their China Dream. This dream was a combination of material prosperity and spiritual satisfaction deriving from living in a country that had been restored to its status and its core role in the world. For Xi in his 2017 speech, that dream was of a society that was innovative, where the creative energies of the Chinese people, liberated by the country's good education system, were now equal – and in many respects superior – to the world around them. There would be no more reliance on foreign technology and know-how; the era would be done with learning from the rest of the world because of a massive domestic knowledge deficit. Instead, China would be in control of its own advanced technology and would be the destination of envious foreigners, not like a pauper hoping for more of their help.

An innovative China would also be according to Xi a well-governed one, one where the great machinery of administration had finally been perfected and where rules, regulations and protocols according to Chinese characteristics were an ally to stability and an aid to development, and had created an egalitarian society which was truly run on socialist principles. In this society, the temporary acceptance of rising levels of inequality would have finally revealed itself as having been a means to an end – the elevation of the whole of society to a good standard of living. China would have avoided the deep structural flaws of the Western democratic countries, with their huge gaps between rich and poor. It would have delivered modernity to the Chinese countryside, and ensured similar levels of social welfare in both urban and rural areas.

Such a China would be harmonious, a place governed by the hybrid belief systems and philosophies of socialism and traditional Chinese culture. It would be a place of tolerance, where people would be free to practise their religion of choice but also responsible for the society around them, meaning that they would never attempt to give their religious ideas pre-eminence over those of others. It would be a society of justice, where people felt they belonged not just to an equal society but to an equitable one, somewhere with strong civic values where the country was not just a vast collection of discrete familial and individual networks. In this society, there would be no ethnic conflicts as there had been in parts of the US and Europe. There would be satisfaction, contentment and a sense of fulfilment, with people happy in the knowledge they were living in a culture that was deeply rooted, humane and focused on the well-being of the individual.

But it was about more than just the balanced and harmonious relationship between humans. China in 2035 would be a place where humanity lives in concord with nature, and where the environment has finally been cleaned up, carbon emissions are under control, cities are full of green spaces, buildings are built to high ecological standards and the smog that once blighted urban areas is a thing of the past. People would have clean water and good-quality food, and be able to enjoy a natural environment that fills them with inspiration and wonder at the diversity of their great geography.

Further into the future, in 2050, the dream gets even grander and bolder, but more abstract. In its 100th year, the People's Republic will be, in Xi's words, a global leader. It will be fully modernised. It will be prosperous, and democratic, with Chinese characteristics. The dream will have been delivered. The great rejuvenation of the Chinese nation will have been achieved. And at that point the Party will be able to justify the arduous struggle of the last two centuries as a vital step on the way to realising this ambition; the role of the people will simply have been to keep on believing in their dreams and in the grand plans of the Communist Party of China. As long as they have kept the faith over the years, then they will see all those dreams come true.

This is an intoxicating vision, and all the more so because it is based on more than just speculation. Since 1949, the Party has delivered on many of its promises – such as unity and greater international respect and credibility for China. Mao was the vision man, the boldest dreamer of all. But his utopian visions lacked any sense of pragmatic strategy, and the China he created was afflicted by internal trauma and fragmentation. Deng was the more prosaic thinker, but the greater strategist of the two. His great insight was that without material wealth, China's great national dream would never proceed. Shifting the sole focus of government and society to the creation of wealth proved a stroke of genius. For over three decades, it kept the narrative simple in a complex society.

By 2012, China's economic and material capital was massive. Quicker and more effectively than anyone had ever expected, it had become the world's second-largest economy. Xi Jinping therefore came to the leadership during a time of plenty, and faced a period of fundamental choice. Now China was powerful and wealthy, how did it want to use its new-found prominence and status? For Xi, the choice has been dictated not by the present or the future, but by the past: his leadership has always been obliged to deliver the great dream – the promise made decades before the Party even existed, let alone came to power. The hope had always been to deliver a strong, rich, powerful country. But under Xi, this goal was no longer centuries or decades away – it was imminent, just over the horizon. People could reach out and feel it, touch it, taste it and see it. For this China, Xi is the enabler and leader who can tell the story as it happens. History has been kind to him so far, allowing him to build on the legacy of others. His only responsibility is to make sure that he gets things right. For that reason, there is a powerful sense of caution about everything he does.

Whatever people might think of the system he presides over, and its expressions of power and authority, there must be some level of recognition in China that he has been proven right so far on the issue of how he and his fellow leaders have read the national mood. Chinese people might care very little for Xi Jinping Thought; certainly, they were largely indifferent to him being accorded the title of 'Core Leader' in 2016. But his articulation of a national aspiration – and his enforcement of discipline and purpose in the Party to achieve this – has proved popular. At a time when the world is afflicted by the cruel mockery of a Trump presidency and its anti-idealism, or of European leaders afflicted by lack of confidence and popular dissatisfaction, Xi stands in a different place. He dares to speak about dreams and about ideal outcomes, and about a beautiful future. It would be mean and ungenerous to want to deny Chinese people their moment of regeneration. In the end, their aspirations and hopes are the real autocrats of modern China. Xi is merely the servant of these. And as long as he is seen to be delivering these goals, his leadership will be secure.

POSTSCRIPT

WHAT HAPPENS TO LUCKY MEN WHEN THE LUCK RUNS OUT?

There is a saying in modern British politics that all polit-ical careers end in failure. Tony Blair was elected in 1997 with one of the largest landslides in British voting history, nearly duplicating this four years later. It seemed for a long time that he was able to walk on water. The oppo-sition were in disarray. The major newspapers supported him. He dominated his own party. The only thorn in his side was the clear jealousy of his closest colleague, Gordon Brown. But for a decade, Blair reigned supreme.

These days, the former British prime minister wan-ders the world giving highly paid speeches, some of them in China. His influence in his homeland is close to nil. His involvement in support for George W. Bush in the second Iraq War, which began in 2003, effectively destroyed his reputation. The man who once looked to be on top of the world is now mostly regarded as being buried under it.

Blair was the product of electoral multiparty systems; it would be incorrect to present him to Xi Jinping as a kind of memento mori. But there is one salient lesson to be drawn from his demise, and that is that luck comes and goes. And Xi Jinping is probably the luckiest man in China – perhaps even the world.

He is lucky for two main reasons. The first is that he has arrived at a point in China's story where it has never been more favoured in terms of its wealth and influence. This has not been his creation, but that of the Chinese people and the leaders who have preceded him. The main achievement under Mao, broadly speaking, was national reunification: he ended the era of division and fragmentation. China would never have been able to stand up if both its legs had been missing, which was in effect the case before 1949. After this time, despite Mao's colossal mistakes, the country's unity was never seriously questioned. Even during the Cultural Revolution, when at times China looked dangerously close to returning to civil war, disunity was only ever a remote possibility. Under Deng, the calculation was made that without economic and material strength, China's future would never truly be secure. An immense effort was made to generate this wealth – and it succeeded. Jiang and Hu continued that trajectory. Jiang in particular dealt with the fallout of the post-1989 crisis and the impact of the collapse of the Soviet Union. Hu simply focused relentlessly on growth.

Xi inherits a unified country with a dynamic economy, where the Communist Party remains dominant. He is stewarding it towards the imminent moment when it will again become a great nation – 2021. All China's stars are aligned. His one duty is not to screw things up, rather than to be proactive, and that is what he seems to be attempting to do.

Even more striking is the complete lack of viable opponents within the Party to oppose him. Mao had to deal with endless potential competitors. Some, like Gao Gang, he dealt with brutally. Others, like Zhou Enlai, he initially co-opted and turned into allies. Throughout his life, he faced opponents – from Marshal Peng Dehuai, who was the main critic of his Great Leap Forward policies, to the champions of greater market liberalisation in the early 1960s. Deng Xiaoping was one of these, and when his chance came to exercise real influence, he was only able to do so after huge amounts of negotiation and work within the party elite. Chen Yun was a particularly vocal and powerful defender of much less accelerated market reforms in the 1980s. In the 1990s, Deng as an octogenarian had to face down conservatives who took the events of 1989 as their chance to put pressure on the Party to retrench and return to more orthodox Maoism. His famous Southern Tour during 1991 and 1992 was the answer to this.

Jiang and Hu were also not given an easy run. Jiang had to build his reputation as a leader in the face of a sceptical Party elite who felt he was the least impressive candidate, and had the formidable talents of his premier Zhu Rongji to manage, rather than succumb to. In addition, there were still members of the old guard lingering around him, even after Deng's death. Hu Jintao had to fight throughout his period of leadership against the continuing influence of the man who never seemed to go away – his predecessor Jiang Zemin!

Xi Jinping has been handed as close as one can get to a clean slate. The only viable source of opposition to him managed – in a stroke of marvellous good fortune for Xi – to be removed shortly before the 18th Party Congress. Bo Xilai, the handsome, charismatic, popular and daring princeling, was a real alternative, even though he had not been promoted in 2007. He would have been a potential lightning conductor who could have distracted from Xi by using policies eerily similar to the ones that Xi was to use after 2012.

Only those most wedded to conspiracy theories would accept that Bo's felling was manufactured by Xi or those wishing to see him as leader; no one could have predicted the events of 2011 that would lead to Bo's wife being arrested for murder in early 2012, as discussed in Chapter 1. This completely removed from the frame the one opponent who might potentially have taken some of the shine from Xi. Without Bo's presence, Xi dominates with no distractions.

These two generous 'gifts' mean that Xi is the king of luck, whatever else he may be. There is no question that he has used his luck well, but it leaves nagging questions about just how able he might be to deal with real challenges like those of his predecessors. Were there a scenario like in 1989, with mass uprisings, would he hold his nerve? Would he be able to respond as Deng did: ruthlessly, heedless of international pressure and with an iron grip on the military? Or would he dither, delay, negotiate and run the risk of seeing the Communist Party of China go the same way as that of the USSR? What about an economic downturn, unexpected and sharp? Would he have the steel to respond as Hu and Wen Jiabao did a decade before and pump vast amounts into the economy to stave off a recession? Would he mandate the use of utterly unorthodox means in order to preserve the things that needed to be preserved – the unity and protection of the one-party rule?

We have not experienced what Xi is like as a crisis leader because, remarkably, the China of today has had a number of years of stability, both domestically and externally. Despite the tensions with North Korea, and in the South and East China Seas, the parlous state of the US and much of the rest of the world means that China is too important a country to fail. We are all stakeholders in Xi's leadership, and in its success. The collapse of China used to be, in the era of Mao, a real likelihood. Today it would bring about Armageddon. Global supply chains, capital flows and security would be undermined, perhaps fatally. The pillar of stability in the most critical region for growth in the world would be eroded, leading to a tsunami of knock-on effects across the rest of the world. It is no longer a question of containing China; China now contains us. Its failure would be ours.

For this reason, Xi is a global leader. His responses, especially if a crisis were ever to arise, would be crucial for everyone. His instincts on North Korea, on managing the capricious Trump presidency, on handling issues in the Asia region, and on having an influence over Africa and the Middle East will make the difference between failure and success. If he takes a misstep, the consequences will be calamitous. Seeing him as just another staid Politburo leader with dyed hair ponderously wandering the planet buried in protocol would be a massive mistake. He is far more than that. This lucky man will need massive guile, vision and resilience when the luck runs out – as it always does. The question of whether he has the qualities needed is currently impossible to answer. What is known is that he is from a deeply cautious political culture, and that he has shown himself to be very conservative the few times he has exercised agency in recent years. We should be thankful that the leadership is not as volatile in Beijing as it currently is in Washington.

How does the world view Xi Jinping? For those who have experienced him through newspapers and television reports, he comes across in his visits as an enigma. But then again, Chinese leaders always have been hard to interpret. Hu Jintao's silence left speculators with nothing but air to fill, while Jiang Zemin's play-acting and buffoonery were seen as strategies of intelligence masquerading as folly. Deng was initially embraced as a closet reformer, as though he would suddenly cast off the fact that he had faithfully served the Communist Party through thick and thin since the age of 16. After 1989 he was interpreted as a hard, brutal figure, and the outside world fell out of love with him. And going back further, to Mao, the interpretation was even more extreme: worshipful admiration from those on the left in places like France, a sort of mystical cultural icon for people such as the Beatles, who featured him in one of their songs, but for the rest of the world the epitome of oriental despotism – brutal, cruel, a hate figure.

In the West, we have rarely succeeded in seeing these figures in context – as leaders of a complex, multifaceted country, where even unified Party rule was no more than the calm surface of a lake riddled with deep, turbulent currents and hidden shoals. They were politicians in a world where everything seemed to be about politics, but where Chinese people most of the time (except in the late Mao era) were just trying to get on with their lives. Our focus has always been on the visible life of politics – not the deeper China that lies all around, with its ancient history, its layered society, its unending social and cultural complexity. Chinese leaders were symbolic of this deeper China. But this granted them a reach, and a power, that they never really had. The China story was never really about them; instead, it was about the nation they were trying to represent. And that has never been an easy task.

In this era of ambition, and of social networks and instantaneous communication, Xi is the leader whose personality has to encapsulate all these different elements. Somehow he has to speak to an outside world that either wants the impossible from China – through investment, capital and market access that will make them rich – or sees it as the new enemy. In December 2017, despite the smiles and pleasantries during his visit to Beijing just a month before, Donald Trump described China in a security review as a strategic competitor. About the same time, at a cybersecurity forum in London, I heard experts from Europe and the US brush off potential problems from Russia and elsewhere and name the People's Republic as the main threat. 'They are drawing blood,' one analyst said. One could almost hear the sabres, albeit virtual ones, rattling in the conference hall.

Xi travels extensively, and on his visits he smiles and speaks to the rest of the world reassuringly. He says – and he is right on this front – that China, at least since 1979, has never engaged in any act of military combat. He says that a strong China, a secure China, is a source of global stability and a good thing. He is right also when he says that ensuring the welfare of a fifth of humanity is a massive task – and the Chinese government has been doing this since 1978, or at least allowing this to happen. But people are getting spooked by the ways that the Chinese state operates. In Australia and New Zealand, fears of political infiltration are almost reaching fever pitch. The highly admired former Australian ambassador to China (and current head of the diplomatic service), Frances Adamson, stated crisply in a seminar in late 2017 that Australians should never compromise their values to an invasive, insidious Chinese state-led external campaign. In New Zealand, it was claimed that Yang Jian, a popular MP in the 2017 election who originally hailed from China, was a former spy and member of the Communist Party who had never fully declared his background.

These counter-narratives to those promoted by Xi show the complexity of the world that China faces. India might be all smiles sometimes, but it is evidently uneasy about the ambitions behind the Belt and Road Initiative. In the US and EU, suspicions about rising levels of Chinese investment grow stronger by the day, increasing along with the volumes of money coming in.

China has set out its narrative, through the China Dream and the Belt and Road Initiative. But the counter-narratives from the West are troubling. Everywhere you look, people find different things to distrust. There are, to coin a phrase, 50 shades of fear. Xi is the person who can try and assuage these fears. But everything about him – his background, his way of operating, the power that emanates from him and his entourage – reinforces the very messages he is meant to negate.

Whatever people feel about Xi and the kind of culture he comes from, there is one thing that is undeniable – at least politically. No one outside China has any right, moral or otherwise, to deny the nation Xi leads its moment of fulfilment. It should be a cause of global celebration that a country once riddled with and crippled by poverty, disease and discord is now stable, wealthy, healthy and a contributor, rather than a taker. The historic mission that Xi talked about in mid-October may be more stirring to Chinese people than those outside the country, but when you think back to the abyss of suffering that China came from less than a century ago, only the least fair-minded would begrudge China its renaissance. The country paid a terrible price to be where it is today. Xi might not matter much to us as the leader of a one-party system we dislike and wish to see reformed. But as the servant of this China that brings justice, historic redemption and hope, he appears in a different guise. We should never forget the unpalatable facts about the reality of the Chinese state today, which have already been touched upon in this book. But we must also never forget the other reality, that of a country that has risen from the ashes of war, famine and fragmentation to become a global force again. China's story is complicated, but it is also a truthful one. And the key issue for global engagement with Xi's China is how capable we are in the West of embracing this complexity. In that crucial sense, Xi's China is also our China. We are part of the story too – whether we like it or not.

SUGGESTED READING

The speeches and talks of Xi Jinping have been well translated into English, and are in the two-volume *The Governance of China* (Beijing: Foreign Languages Press, 2015 and 2017). The full text of his first speech as General Secretary of the Communist Party in Beijing in 2012 can also be found on the BBC News website: http://www.bbc.com/news/world-asia-china-20338586. Xi's speech at the 2017 Congress, which has been heavily referred to in this work, is available in English translation at the *China Daily* website: http://www.chinadaily.com.cn/china/19th-cpcnationalcongress/2017-11/04/content_34115212.htm.

For Xi himself, the main English-language works are my own *CEO, China: The Rise of Xi Jinping* (London: I.B.Tauris, 2016) and veteran China watcher Willy Wo-Lap Lam's *Chinese Politics in the Era of Xi Jinping: Renaissance, Reform, or Retrogression?* (London: Routledge, 2015).

INDEX